PUTTING KIDS FIRST IN DIVORCE

How to Reduce Conflict, Preserve
Relationships & Protect Your Children During
& After Divorce

PUTTING KIDS FIRST IN DIVORCE

How to Reduce Conflict, Preserve Relationships & Protect Your Children
During & After Divorce
[Even If You're Dealing with an Antagonistic Ex]

Jeremy S. Kossen, Mark B. Baer, Esq., Karen Bonnell, ARNP, MS, Amanda D. Singer, Esq., MDR, CDFA™, Jennifer M. Segura, JD, CDFA™, Belinda N. Zylberman, JD, Kristine Clay, MA, Maida V. Farrar, Esq., CDC, Nicola Beer, Sara Freed, Cherie D. Morris

MOGULY MEDIA

Publishing support, design, and composition by Moguly Media, LLC, Building Brands Authoritatively

www.mogulymedia.com

Publisher's Note:
Book Layout © 2014 BookDesignTemplates.com

TABLE OF CONTENTS

Thank you for purchasing DivorceBuddy.co's "Putting Kids First," published by Moguly Media.

To receive other great divorce content from high integrity professionals, such as new blog posts, podcast episodes, book launches, and (soon) online courses, sign up for the DivorceBuddy.co newsletter: www.divorcebuddy.co/newsletter

DEDICATION

To my beautiful children, Chloe Rose and Griffin Asher, whose brilliance and compassion inspire me through life's peaks and valleys. Je t'adore;

To Kaitlin and Jake, wise beyond your years, always continue to pause and reflect, and seek the path that asserts integrity of purpose and imaginative vision;

To Andy, and those whose work has greatly influenced my thinking;

Melissa Farrar, who is both the shooting star and the moon in the trees;

Cameron, Julia, Grayson, Annabelle and to my bonus child, Sophia;

Nanny Rose who brought happiness, laughter and love through our difficult childhood;

Mordechai T., Esther, and Yoseph, I am so proud of the adults you have become and look forward to seeing even more success in your future;

Dedicated to the little people that make our life colorful, Marley Jean, Cedella Schade and Sienna M.;

To those who inspired it, and will not read it;

To all parents who have committed to set aside their own conflict and struggle, and focus on the unique and specific needs of their children as their family goes through transition;

To all the brave and loving parents who find their way to work together to preserve their children's one-and-only childhood as they restructure their family.

Co-Parents' Credo: I won't let the mistakes and failures of our marriage tumble forward and become the mistakes and failures of our co-parenting. This I commit to you and to our children.

A Note on Hiring Divorce Professionals

Putting Kids First in Divorce features a diverse cross-section of contributors with experience spanning family law, mediation, collaborative law, therapy, counseling, and coaching. In this book, we outline strategies on how to minimize conflict and stay out of court. As you read this book and begin interviewing professionals, it's important to understand the distinctions between the different types of professionals you may work with during this process.

Every professional is unique and possesses an outlook and approach shaped by their own individual experiences. No individual professional can be all things to all people. So, just because a professional is appropriate for one of your friends or family members, does not mean they are the best choice for you. Further, one's degrees or credentials are not in and of themselves predictors of whether they are right for your situation, nor should you hire a professional solely based on them. While these are important factors, there are other criteria you should also consider.

Do they share common experiences with you? Do they share your values? How much experience do they have working with people who are dealing with circumstances similar to ones you are experiencing? Do they have experience working with individuals who share similar characteristics with your soon-to-be-ex? These are all important questions to consider.

Further, you may come across professionals who include mediation or collaborative law in their practice areas. However, upon closer scrutiny, you may find that the bulk of their practice centers around litigation. Likewise, you may come across a divorce coach who lacks the experience, education or credentials that qualified coaches may have. (In Chapter Two, we provide a list of questions you may ask a mediator or collaborative law professional. Many of these questions are appropriate—or may be adapted—to use when you evaluate other professionals.)

Below, we outline the role of the various types of professionals we reference in the book:

Divorce Coach

The role of a divorce coach is to help you navigate your divorce and support you. They focus on the present and future with practical solutions and actionable strategies, without delving heavily into the past. Although many divorce coaches have family law or mental health backgrounds, in their role as a coach, they are neither your attorney nor therapist. However, they can often be an invaluable resource to help you find a good therapist if you need one, and even helping you find a good mediator or collaborative divorce practitioner.

The American Bar Association defines personal divorce coaching as follows:

> Divorce coaching is a flexible, goal-oriented process designed to support, motivate, and guide people going through divorce to help them make the best possible decisions for their future, based on their particular interests, needs, and concerns. Divorce coaches have different professional backgrounds and are selected based on the specific needs of the clients. For example, some divorce coaches are financial planners, mental health professionals, lawyers, or mediators who have experience dealing with divorcing clients.

Note that the ABA explains divorce coaching is flexible, goal-oriented and designed to support and motivate you so that you can make the best possible decisions for your future. However, most coaches will not advise you on legal issues or provide you with therapy, as they are not operating as an attorney or therapist; therefore protections against forced disclosure do not apply. While this rarely presents an issue, if you fear your soon-to-be-ex will litigate, use common sense and don't share information that could be used against you in court. Information or details you deem highly confidential or personal should be shared only with a professional bound by confidentiality or privileged communications protections. A good coach respects legal and ethical boundaries, and will be helpful in redirecting you towards the appropriate professional when necessary.

As you evaluate coaches, consider their particular background and personal experience. Most do share a common experience in that they have been personally affected by divorce, either their own or parent's divorce—or both. They will assist you to design a process tailored to your personal situation and geared towards maximizing your potential. However, you play a vital role and are responsible for following the process. Again, coaches focus on the present and future. Unlike certain aspects of therapy, a coach does not provide treatment designed to "heal" past issues.

To find a certified divorce coach, you may find CDC Certified Divorce Coach® helpful.

Therapist

Distinct from coaching, the role of a therapist is diagnostic and treatment based. Their role is often complementary to coaching. However, because a therapist's role is, by defini-tion, therapeutic, they may be able to support you in ways that other professionals can't. Divorce may contribute to or exacerbate certain mental health conditions including depression, anxiety, or personality disorders. A qualified therapist can help you deal with many of the emotional struggles you may encounter in your divorce—feelings of fear, anxiety, guilt, grief or depression. Your therapist can provide a rational and objective perspective while equipping you with critical skills to overcome these difficulties.

Therapy can help you make sense of your divorce, gain new perspective—even help you learn what you do or don't want in future relationships. Through therapy, you may be able to learn more about yourself, even finding peace and solace through the experience. A good therapist can help you find opportunities for personal growth and development. Therapy can help one work through their feelings, make sense of the end of the marriage, and obtain a new perspective.

Going through a divorce can be one of the most stressful and emotionally traumatic events in one's life. Don't be afraid of reaching out to a therapist during this time, as they can be an invaluable asset during times of distress.

To find a therapist, you may find Psychology Today or the American Association for Marriage and Family Therapists helpful.

Mediator & Collaborative Divorce Practitioners

In Chapter Two, you will gain a solid understanding of the roles and responsibilities of Mediators and Collaborative Divorce Practitioners; why most divorcing couples find cooperative divorce methods more valuable than litigation; and, how to find and evaluate the appropriate professional or professionals for you or your situation. As an introduction, you can find a brief overview and description of each role as defined by the American Bar Association:

Mediation:

Mediation is a private process where a neutral third person called a mediator helps the parties discuss and try to resolve the dispute. The parties have the opportunity to describe the issues, discuss their interests, understandings, and feelings; provide each other with information and explore ideas for the resolution of the dispute. While courts can mandate that certain cases go to mediation, the process remains "voluntary" in that the parties are not required to come to agreement.

The mediator does not have the power to make a decision for the parties, but can help the parties find a resolution that is mutually acceptable. The only people who can resolve the dispute in mediation are the parties themselves.

There are a number of different ways that a mediation can proceed. Most mediations start with the parties together in a joint session. The mediator will describe how the process works, will explain the mediator's role and will help establish ground rules and an agenda for the session.

Some mediators conduct the entire process in a joint session. However, other mediators will move to separate sessions, shuttling back and forth between the parties. If the parties reach an agreement, the mediator may help reduce the agreement to a written contract, which may be enforceable in court.

Collaborative Law:

Collaborative Law of Collaborative Practice is an out-of-court settlement process where parties and their lawyers try to reach an agreement satisfying the needs of all parties and any children involved. The parties agree to provide all relevant information. If the parties engage in contested litigation, their Collaborative lawyers cannot represent them in court. The process typically involves "four-way meetings" with the parties and lawyers and possibly other professionals such as neutral financial specialists, communications coaches, child specialists, or appraisers.

Final Note & Disclaimer

The goal of this book is to help you make informed decisions on how to navigate your divorce. Our goal (and hope) is that you choose cooperative measures rather than combative ones. However, keep in mind that the information provided in this book is for informational purposes only and not for the purpose of providing legal advice. Before making any significant decisions that could impact your future, you should first consult your attorney to obtain advice on particular issues or problems. Finally, the opinions expressed in this book are the opinions of the individual contributors and may not reflect the opinions of the publisher or other individual contributors.

If Divorce Were a Game

> *"Outcomes are typically determined by the way in which the 'game' is designed." —Mark Baer*

If divorce were a game, you might describe it like the game we grew up with: *Monopoly*.

Who doesn't remember the objective of *Monopoly?* Dominate and defeat your adversaries by driving them into bankruptcy. Sound familiar?

In *Monopoly,* the winner is the lucky monopolist who is left with control of the entire economy. Like the game, the divorce process was built on a win/lose paradigm. It's court. You're suing each other. The perception is: one party wins; one party loses. However, unlike *Monopoly*, the game is rigged, and it's not one of the parties who wins. The only one who can win the game is "the system." The system is family court and its financial beneficiaries—principally attorneys, judges and other "conflict profiteers." Sadly, there are many more losers: you, your ex, your children, among others.

Like *Monopoly*, the winner in divorce—the system or monopolist—controls the entire economy. But unlike *Monopoly*, litigation isn't very fun. From the outset, it's adversarial. When you go to court, you make demands; you face orders. The more you fight, the more money your attorneys make. You willingly cede control of your life and your future. You're rolling the dice.

If one wanted to create a game that fuels conflict—instead of resolving it—could you think of a better way? This game doesn't sound very fun or fair, does it? It's not!

Why would you choose to play a game in which the odds are not only stacked against you, but fixed so that you have no chance of (truly) winning?

Sure, you may be able to quit the game after you start playing, but once you start playing, like Vegas, it's hard to quit when you're down—or up.

Why not play a different game from the outset? A game that was designed to:

Minimize conflict, not exacerbate it.

Provide you with choices that allow you to control the outcome.

Save you (a lot of) money, emotional turmoil, and pain.

Put your children's interest first.

And, most importantly, a game in which you preserve your relationships, dignity, and sanity.

Fortunately, such a "game' exists. For fun, let's call it *Co-opoly*, or "cooperative divorce." Instead of hiring an aggressive family law attorney, *you* may choose who you work with and what your team looks like: mediators, collaborative law professionals, therapists, and coaches (divorce, relationship or life).

The pages you are about to read in this book, *Putting Kids First*, are filled with wisdom and actionable strategies developed by professionals who embody the "cooperative" spirit of *Co-opoly*. We are a diverse group of professionals who are passionate about empowering parents with the ability to control their destiny and navigate divorce in a sensible, non-adversarial way.

In writing *Putting Kids First,* we assembled an inspiring group of coaches, mediators, and therapists, who came together with a common mission: help parents approach divorce in a manner that minimizes conflict and puts kids first. We believe passionately that parents should never lose site of the fact that even after divorce, a co-parenting relationship will continue to exist, and how we decide to approach divorce will influence what this co-parenting relationship will look like. You can choose *Monopoly* or *Co-opoly*—Combat or Cooperation. If we choose the former—the litigious path—it's hard to undo or repair much of the damage that litigation-fueled conflict creates. Conversely, if we choose a cooperative child-centric approach to divorce, we will benefit, and so will our children.

Our hope is that you find this book to be uplifting and inspirational, that by reading it, you feel empowered with the knowledge and tools to navigate divorce in the most amicable way. And, of course, put your kids first!

Sage Words of Advice to Parents from Family Court Judge

Dear Parents:

Your children have come into this world because of the two of you. Perhaps you two made lousy choices as to whom you decided to be the other parent. If so, that is your problem and your fault.

No matter what you think of the other party—or what your family thinks of the other party—these children are one=half of each of you. Remember that, because every time you tell your child what an "idiot" his father is, or what a "fool" his mother is, or how bad the absent parent is, or what terrible things that person has done, you are telling the child half of him is bad.

That is an unforgivable thing to do to a child. That is **not love**. That is **possession.** If you do that to your children, you will destroy them as surely as if you had cut them into pieces, because that is what you are doing with their emotions.

I sincerely hope that you do not do that to your children. Think more about your children and less about yourselves, and make yours a selfless kind of love, not foolish or selfish, or your children will suffer.

Judge Michael Haas, 2001

CHAPTER ONE

Choose Cooperation Over Combat

by Jeremy S. Kossen And Mark B. Baer

> *"Conflict cannot survive without your participation."*
> *— Dr. Wayne Dyer*

Children need parents who are bigger than their problems, which is no easy task for parents who are divorcing. It takes grit to give children what they need by taking a psychologically-minded and child-centered approach to your divorce. You deserve praise for wanting to take such an approach for your children's sake.

During a divorce, it's easy to let your emotions get the best of you. For any number of reasons, many parents choose to handle their divorce like a war. However, a battlefield is no place for children, and the decision to divorce in such a manner is almost never in your child's best interest. By opting to read this book, you've made a conscious decision to approach your divorce with mindfulness and sensitivity to your children's needs.

In this chapter, you will learn how to create a cooperative divorce, instead of a combative one. While we will be referring to divorcing parents, this information applies equally well to parents who are separating or otherwise ending their romantic relationship (assuming they ever had one). By the end of this chapter, you should have a solid understanding of the following concepts:

- Why starting with the end goal in mind helps to reduce conflict and maintain focus on the bigger picture

- Viewing divorce from a child's perspective

- What harms children and how to protect them from harm

- How ongoing conflict can cause more harm to children than the divorce itself

- The importance of distinguishing parental "wants" from children's "needs"

- Recognizing "subconscious bias" and developing self-awareness

Start With The End Goal in Mind

It takes two people to agree to marry and only one to decide to divorce. Regardless of how you've come to divorce and who made that decision, it likely wasn't something taken lightly and the underlying causes didn't occur overnight. Conflict and emotions, often elevated during a divorce, tend to cloud our judgment. You may feel hurt, scared, angry, even betrayed. You may even have conscious (or subconscious) desire to punish your soon-to-be-ex. It's important not to inappropriately act on these feelings, as they may lead you to make decisions that feel good at the moment—but, in the end, hurt your children.

It's long been said: "you may win a fight, but lose a relationship." In fact, it may have played a role in your arriving at this place. However, like it or not, when a couple has children together (regardless of their age), their family still exists after the marriage ends. Your parental relationship doesn't end along with the dissolution of your union. Therefore, consider whom a loss of your co-parent relationship harms most. When children are involved, you can't "win" a divorce or aspects of a divorce, regardless of how you believe such a "win" may feel. That feeling is typically short-lived, and the win-lose paradigm in a divorce tends not serve your or your children's best interests in the long run.

A divorce doesn't end the chronic conflict between two people who will be tied together for life through their children. For the benefit of your kids, doesn't it make more sense to resolve or otherwise manage conflict with your ex, than to exacerbate it?

Surprisingly, it can be easier than you think if you're willing to learn from other people's mistakes. As you embark on this journey, consider the following questions:

How many parents do you think have no regrets about how they approached their divorce?

If given the opportunity, how many people would have done things differently?

Do most people look back on their divorce and think they should have spent more money on lawyers, been angrier with their ex, or engaged in more conflict?

Why do people so often ignore the lessons from others' mistakes and make decisions that negatively impact their future? Simple. When a parent operates from a position of anger or resentment, predictably, they disregard the indelible impact their decisions have on their children. No loving parent wants to inflict pain on their children, but they often unintentionally do just that. The satisfaction a parent may experience through short-sighted decisions is no more than instant gratification—choosing that immediate sensation over the long-term consequences. Instead, consider a long view of what you want your life to look like.

Three, five, or ten years from now, do you want a life filled with:

- Conflict and animosity
- High-stress
- Regrets

Or, do you want to have a life in which:

- You can—if not be friends with your ex—at least be civil and cooperative
- Your actions and behaviors provide positive modeling for your children
- Your children are well-adjusted, happy and free of resentment because you acted in alignment with their interests and needs.

When going through a divorce filled with chronic conflict, how do we manage our emotions and control our behaviors in ways that ensure our children endure as little pain as possible? Start with the end goal in mind: not a month or a year from now, but many years from now.

To help you align your actions with your personal values and long-term goals, visualize the ideal co-parenting relationship and how it would look three, five, or ten years down the road. Then document this vision in writing. Save your writing somewhere you can easily access for future reference. It is, in essence, your vision statement. When your co-parent does something that angers you (or you're feeling frustrated), before you react, re-read your vision statement. As you contemplate how to respond, ask yourself how that would align with your personal values and long-term goals.

View Divorce Through Your Child's Perspective

When immersed in emotional turmoil, as is often the case in divorce, it's easy to forget that your children are unique individuals who may interpret things differently than you. Therefore, it's crucial to put yourself in your children's shoes and view your divorce from their perspective—recognize their needs. To do so requires empathy.

What is empathy and why is it important? Brené Brown, Ph.D., LMSW, a best-selling author and research professor who studies vulnerability, courage, worthiness, and shame, believes empathy is a skill set and that perspective taking is at its core. Perspective taking is normally taught or modeled by parents, which makes your doing so that much more important. Dr. Brown contends that we can't take off the lens from which we see the world. We all view it differently, based on our information, insight, and experiences. Moreover, Dr. Brown suggests:

> *Perspective taking is listening to the truth as other people experience it and acknowledging it as the truth.* What you see is as true, real and honest as what I see, so let me be quiet for a minute, listen and learn about what you see. Let me get curious about what you see. Allow me to ask questions about what you see.

> *Empathy is incompatible with shame and judgment.* Staying out of judgment requires understanding. We tend to judge those areas where we're the most vulnerable to feeling shame ourselves. We don't tend to judge others in areas where our sense of self-worth is stable and secure. In order to stay out of judgment, we must pay attention to our own triggers and issues.

> *Empathy reduces shame, whereas sympathy exacerbates it.* There is a huge difference between feeling with someone and feeling for someone. Shame causes a person to believe they're alone. Through

empathy, we cause them to realize that they are not alone, which is why it is the antidote to shame. As Dr. Brown said in her book, *I Thought It Was Just Me*, "In most cases, when we provide sympathy we do not reach across to understand the world as others see it. We look at others from our world and feel sorry or sad for them. Inherent in sympathy is 'I don't understand your world, but from this view, things look pretty bad.'"

When you can see things from your children's perspective, you are better able to deal with your divorce not from a place of anger or a desire for retribution, but from an emotionally healthier place in which you put your children's emotional needs first.

How You Choose to Approach Divorce Impacts Children More Than Divorce Itself

No matter how you slice it, divorce is hard on children. Children are harmed by a sense of helplessness, lack of predictability, parental conflict, poor parenting, and poverty. It's important to understand that parental conflict and unpredictability lead to poor parenting and perpetuate feelings of helplessness in children. Likewise, chronic conflict lends itself to protracted and ongoing litigation causing children significant emotional distress.

The good news, however, is that you have the power to approach your divorce in a way that reduces conflict; you can choose to collaborate with each other instead of competing against each other. By exposing children to less conflict, they will suffer less and recover far more easily. It's interesting to note that children are often better off with divorced parents who get along and put their children's needs and interests first, than with parents who remain in bad marriages and expose them to chronic parental conflict.

Research conducted in recent years demonstrates that when parents choose cooperation over conflict, the negative effects of divorce on children are less severe than previously thought. In fact, researchers view chronic parental conflict, more than the divorce itself, as the most defining factor influencing how a child adjusts after divorce.

According to Stephen Ross, PsyD, HSPP, a child's psychological reaction to their parents' divorce varies in degree, depending upon the following three factors:

1. The quality of their relationship with each of their parents before the separation

2. The intensity and duration of the parental conflict

3. The parents' ability to focus on the needs of children throughout their divorce

According to Dr. Ross, "The key component of these three aspects is that the parents do everything they can to make decisions during the divorce process which are intended to enhance the quality of life for their children rather than trying to punish the other parent."

Ross states that such punishment may take the form of "intended or unintended derogatory comments made within earshot of the child." He says that, "[E]ven subtle nonverbal cues can send a message to a child, e.g. smirking when speaking about the other parent. Children are quite astute in reading nonverbal cues."

Gary Direnfeld, a marriage and family therapist and recognized expert on parent-child relations and child development, agrees: "The greater the conflict between the parents, the greater the risk for a poor outcome for the child. The degree to which parents can find reasonable solutions to their differences, the children are better off."

"Parents should do everything they can to make decisions during the divorce process which are intended to enhance the quality of life for their children rather than trying to punish the other parent." - Dr. Stephen Ross

In her book, *Daring Greatly: How the Courage to Be Vulnerable Transforms the Way We Live, Love, Parent, and Lead*, Dr. Brown says:

> Who we are and how we engage with the world are much stronger predictors of how our children will do than what we know about parenting... [W]hat we learn about ourselves and how we learn to engage with the world as children sets a course that either will require us to spend a significant part of our life fighting to reclaim our self-worth or will give us hope, courage, and resilience for our journey...
>
> There's no question that our behavior, thinking, and emotions are hardwired within us and influenced by our environment...When it comes to our sense of love, belonging, and worthiness, we are most radically shaped by our families of origin—what we hear, what we are told, and perhaps most importantly, how we observe our parents engaging with the world... As Joseph Chilton Pearce writes, 'What we *are* teaches the child more than what we say, so we must *be* what we want our children to become.'

The takeaway lesson is: do everything you can to minimize conflict and maximize both your and your co-parent's involvement in your children's lives. Children learn about relationships and many other aspects of life from their parents. Among other things, parents teach their children how to deal with adversity, change, disappointment; children learn from their parents how to handle conflict and solve problems. When children have a strong and engaged relationship with both parents, they feel secure. When children are more secure, they adjust better and recover faster from the adverse effects of divorce.

In *The Co-Parent's Handbook*, Karen Bonnell and Kristin Little capture this point perfectly: "You are one of your children's most valuable and beloved teachers about so many aspects of life. This includes how to face adversity, change, disappointment, and emerge healthy, happy and whole… Children want to love and be loved by both parents freely, without guilt or shame."

Distinguish What You Want Versus What Your Children Need

> *"Dare to be the adults we want our children to be. Who we are and how we engage with the world are much stronger predictors of how our children will do than what we know about parenting… The question isn't so much 'Are you parenting the right way?' as 'Are you the adult you want your child to grow up to be.'" – Brené Brown, Ph.D. LMSW*

When conflict and resentment run high, it's easy for parents to confuse their wants with their children's needs. Parents may use the court system or other means to control or punish each other. While they convince themselves that what they're doing is in their children's best interest, in reality, they are subjecting their children to emotional trauma.

Confusing what a parent wants with what is in their children's best interest is one of the biggest mistakes parents make. Not only are these concepts not one and the same, but the other parent feels the same way about their beliefs. Inevitably, parents' conflation of these concepts leads to increased conflict.

In fact, Bill Eddy, LCSW, JD—lawyer, therapist, mediator and the co-founder and President of the High Conflict Institute—believes, "Much of today's legal disputes are about what I call Emotional Facts—emotionally-generated false information accepted as true and appearing to require emergency legal action."

Keep in mind that regardless of how sincerely you may hold a belief, very often such beliefs are not fact based. The popular Pixar film, *Inside Out*, explores emotions through the character, Riley, a vivacious, hockey-loving 11-year-old Midwestern girl who has her world turned upside down as she attempts to navigate a major life transition. Her emotion (and alter ego), Joy, tells her, "All these facts and opinions look the same. I can't tell them apart." Interestingly, this is the ultimate cause of a great many conflicts in the world, including those leading to divorce and continuing post-separation and divorce.

To distinguish emotional "facts" from actual facts, you may find it helpful to ask yourself the following questions:

What life experiences have led me to feel the way that I do?

What facts would I need to know to enable me to question my point of view?

Further, as you evaluate your beliefs, keep in mind the following definitions:

A fact is something that truly exists or happens; something that has actual existence; a true piece of information.

An opinion is a belief stronger than impression and less strong than positive knowledge.

A belief is a feeling of being sure that someone or something exists or that something is true.

An impression is an idea or belief that is usually not clear or certain.

A feeling is often unreasoned opinion or belief.

(Source: Merriam-Webster's Collegiate® Dictionary)

As you make decisions, beware of your unconscious biases. Research shows that people consistently have incomplete information from which to make decisions and that 99.99% of decision-making is unconscious.

Google initiated an ambitious project called re:Work to study the unconscious mind and raise awareness of "unconscious bias," which they define as "the automatic, mental shortcuts used to process information and make decisions quickly." Their findings are intriguing and are as applicable in the context of the workplace as they are in divorce. They found that unconscious bias can be a "useful [shortcut] when making decisions with limited information, focus, or time." However, it can also, "prevent individuals from making the most objective decisions," and "sometimes lead individuals astray and have unintended consequences."

Fortunately, by understanding unconscious bias and overcoming it at critical moments, we can make better decisions. Google's research finds that "awareness of unconscious bias can lead to reversals in biased outcomes, and understanding the unconscious biases that underlie beliefs may be necessary for changing attitudes."

As you go through your divorce, be aware of unconscious bias and shortcuts you may be tempted to use when making critical decisions; people tend to believe what they want to believe, a concept known as "confirmation bias." Therefore, we must engage in critical thinking to distinguish facts from opinion. (Critical thinking is a concept also addressed in the Pixar film *Inside Out.*) It is the objective analysis and evaluation involved in determining the credibility of any given piece of information, and this determination requires self-awareness.

You may find it beneficial to do more introspection to empathize better with your children and understand that what you think you want as a parent versus what is truly in your children's best interest—these are often very different. It bears mentioning that people who are unwilling to entertain the possibility that their belief on something may be wrong, regardless of what facts may come to light, are closed-minded. Since these kinds of people only care to validate their beliefs, they are inclined to make biased decisions.

Circling back around, Brené Brown observes:

> When it comes to parenting, the practice of framing mothers and fathers as good or bad is both rampant and corrosive—it turns parenting into a shame minefield. The real questions for parents should be: 'Are you engaged? Are you paying attention?' If so, plan to make lots of mistakes and bad decisions. Imperfect parenting moments turn into gifts as our children watch us try to figure out what went wrong and how we can do better next time...

> Engagement means investing time and energy. It means sitting down with our children and understanding their worlds, their interests, and their stories... Engaged parents can be found on both sides of all of the controversial parenting debates. They come from different values, traditions, and cultures. What they share in common is practicing the values. What they seem to share is a

philosophy of 'I'm not perfect and I'm not always right, but I'm here, open, paying attention, loving you, and fully engaged.' There is no question that engagement requires sacrifice, but that's what we signed up for when we decided to become parents.

Always remember that there are different ways to parent children. Parenting styles are a matter of perception. Who's to say that yours is better? 'Better' is in the eye of the beholder. Unless it's something that's endangering your child, it's not the end of the world.

As Dr. Brown says,

> You can't claim to care about the welfare of children if you're shaming other parents for the choices they're making. Those are mutually exclusive behaviors and they create a huge values gap... [I]f we really care about the broader welfare of children, our job is to make choices that are aligned with our values and support other parents who are doing the same. When we feel good about the choices we're making and when we're engaging with the world from a place of worthiness rather than scarcity, we feel no need to judge and attack...

> [The] fact that someone is making different choices from us doesn't in itself constitute abuse. If there's real abuse happening, by all means, call the police. If not, we shouldn't call it abuse. As a social worker who spent a year interning at Child Protective Services, I have little tolerance for debates that casually use the terms *abuse* or *neglect* to scare or belittle parents who are simply doing things that we judge as wrong, different, or bad... The key is remembering that when other parents make different choices than we're making, it's not necessarily criticism...

Compassion and connection—the very things that give purpose and meaning to our lives—can only be learned if they are experienced... Love and belonging are irreducible needs of all men, women, and children. We're hardwired for connection—it's what gives purpose and meaning to our lives... And our families are our first opportunities to experience these things... The absence of love, belonging, and connection always leads to suffering.

For the benefit of your children, the end goal should be to act in ways that support your *children's needs*, not solely *your wants*. When parents aren't ready, willing and able to be bigger than their problems for the sake of their children, it begs the question—why exactly did they have kids in the first place?

Parents are continually presented with choices. And, in divorce, one of the biggest choices you can make is whether to choose a combative or cooperative approach to your divorce. Equipped with an understanding of how these two approaches differ and impact your and your children's lives, you can make an informed decision as to which path makes more sense.

What Factors Motivate Parents to Choose Cooperation Over Combat?

Parents who share common values are typically the most motivated to cooperate with each other. According to Stephen Willis, Ph.D., "Shared values and shared mission are most effective at fostering collaboration."

Encouragingly, the Pew Research Center reported in a survey of families that while parents may differ on a wide range of issues, they share common values on parenting:

- Fully 94% of parents say it is important to teach children responsibility
- Nearly as many—92%—say the same about hard work
- Helpfulness, good manners and independence also are widely viewed as important for children to learn

These findings are wonderful news, considering that "shared values" is the highest motivator for cooperation.

What are the other motivating factors that influence parents' willingness to cooperate?

Shared mission. While every family's "parental mission statement" may differ, certain missions are nearly universal, such as the desire for their children's safety, happiness, sense of worthiness, and emotional well-being.

Family and social bonds. Guess what? Your child's family and social bonds aren't severed by virtue of their parents' divorce.

Common goals. To a large extent, these are going to differ, depending upon the parents' belief systems. However, universally, the highest parental goals are their children's physical survival and health. These goals precede economic self-maintenance and maximization of cultural values.

What are some of the lessons you can draw from these findings?

Strong cooperative motivations exist when people are connected together for life through their children; therefore, when you and your co-parent are introspective, self-aware and open-minded while maintaining focus on the big picture, you can more easily embrace a cooperative paradigm in your divorce. You may have heard the idiom, "You can't see the forest for the trees." It means that when you are too close to a situation you need to step back and get a little perspective—you may be so focused on the many small details, that you have failed to see the overall picture.

Bottom line: If you want to "raise the children you intend to raise," approach your divorce from a place of cooperation in which you work through your conflict, rather than exacerbate it through enmity and competition.

For further resources including DivorceBuddy.co podcasts, visit DivorceBuddy.co.

To learn more about California's "Most Compassionate Mediator", Mark Baer, Esq., visit his website MarkBaerEsq.com. For further reading, visit Mark's Huffington Post Blog, including the following articles:

- Parents Should Think Twice Before Engaging in a Custody Battle Over Their Children

- The Power of Empathy

References:

Bonnell, Karen, and Kristin Little. *The Co-Parents Handbook: Facing Divorce or Separation*. Bloomington, IN: Balboa, 2015. Print.

Brown, Brené. *Daring Greatly: How the Courage to Be Vulnerable Transforms the Way We Live, Love, Parent, and Lead*. Avery Group, 2015. Print.

Eddy, Bill A. *High Conflict People in Legal Disputes*. High Conflict Institute, 2012. Print.

Inside Out. Dir. Pete Docter and Ronnie Del Carmen. Perf. Amy Poehler, Lewis Black and Bill Hader. Pixar Animation Studios, 2015.

Google. "Re:Work - Guide: Raise Awareness about Unconscious Bias." *Re:Work*. 02 Jan. 2016. Web.

Pew Research. "Families May Differ, but They Share Common Values on Parenting." *Pew Research Center*. 2014. Web. 02 Feb. 2016.

Ross, Stephen. "Contested Custody and Its Effects On Children." Web.

Weissbourd, Rick, and Stephanie Jones. *The Children We Mean to Raise: The Real Messages Adults Are Sending About Values*. Rep. Harvard Graduate School of Education, 2014. Web.

Willis, Dr. Stephen. *Power Through Collaboration: The Formula for Success in Challenging Situations*. Willis Consulting (www.PowerThroughCollaboration.com), 2013. Print.

ABOUT JEREMY S. KOSSEN

Jeremy Kossen is the co-founder of DivorceBuddy.co, an e-learning and media company focused on helping parents navigate their divorce in a manner that reduces conflict and lessens potential damage to themselves and loved ones while allowing them to achieve personal growth in the face of adversity. DivorceBuddy.co offers a myriad of resources including blogs, webinars, e-learning courses, and podcasts.

An author and a regular contributor to national and international media, Jeremy immerses himself in his subjects, performing exhaustive research on every topic he covers. He regularly interviews thought leaders and experts on a variety of topic areas, including psychology, politics, technology, film and law. Jeremy feels blessed to be the father of two incredible children, Chloe Rose and Griffin Asher.

Jeremy studied political science and film at the University of California, Los Angeles. He is currently working on several new book and podcast projects.

"We cannot solve our problems with the same thinking we used when we created them." — Albert Einstein

CHAPTER TWO

Stay Out of Court! Choose Mediation or Collaborative Divorce Over Litigation

by Mark B. Baer and Jeremy S. Kossen

> *"Our system is too costly, too painful, too destructive, too inefficient for a truly civilized people. To rely on the adversary process as the principal means of resolving conflicting claims is a mistake that must be corrected." — Warren Berger, former Chief Justice of the United States Supreme Court*

Conflicts of any type can be resolved either through force or diplomacy. In legal disputes, parties try to exert force on each other through the courts. "We call it an adversary system, but a better term would be a coercion system. The parties bash each other to persuade the judge to coerce the other person to do something they do not want to do," says Family Court Judge Bruce Peterson of Hennepin County, Minneapolis. The threat of having a judge coerce "a person to do something they do not want to do" unless they agree to certain terms is itself coercive.

The litigation process, which is based on a "win-lose" paradigm, is not conducive to situations involving an ongoing relationship, such as the relationship between parents tied together for life through their children.

Typically, a divorce occurs due to marital discord, and litigation exacerbates whatever conflict already exists. When the matter is finally "resolved," is it any surprise that the parties find themselves unable to co-parent—or that they violate coerced "agreements" or court orders? The reason the word "resolved" has quotation marks around it is that a case is not over once the judge signs the final divorce decree. While the parties may have received a legal answer to their dispute through a judicial order or agreement obtained through threat of such an order, the emotional conflict between them has by no means been "resolved."

And if that's not bad enough, family law cases are considered the vampires of the legal field because of the ongoing legal rematches on any and all issues left open for possible future modification for legitimate public policy reasons. Such issues may involve parenting plans and timeshare arrangements (child custody and visitation), child support, and modifiable spousal support (alimony).

Diplomacy, on the other hand, works through mediation, collaborative law, and other forms of Consensual Dispute Resolution (CDR). As the name implies, the parties to such processes resolve their conflicts through mutual consent, without obtaining such consent through coercion.

Consensus building and litigation could not be more different. Litigation increases hostility, breeds paranoia, worsens emotional wounds and further damages family dynamics. Consensus building, on the other hand, is designed to de-escalate conflict and rebuild trust, thereby enabling the parties to resolve their issues through cooperative means.

The conventional wisdom is that when a couple divorces, they must embrace the adversarial "win-lose" paradigm typical of the Family Court process. As you will learn from this chapter, this couldn't be further from the truth. Every couple has a choice. They can allow the courts to decide their future—and in the process cause potentially irreparable emotional harm to themselves and their children—or pursue a "child-centric" cooperative approach by using true mediation or a collaborative divorce process.

By the end of this chapter, you should have solid understanding of the following concepts:

- Why cooperative methods to divorce, such as mediation or collaborative law, are typically superior to litigation

- How Family Court is inherently adversarial

- How attorneys can be part of the solution or part of the problem

- The benefits of and key differences between mediation and collaborative divorce

- Whether a cooperative divorce is possible in a high-conflict—or potentially high-conflict—divorce

- How to hire the most suitable mediation or collaborative divorce professionals

Let's first examine litigation—or what we call, combative divorce—the process you want to do everything possible to avoid:

Combative Divorce

Litigation. Adversarial. Conflict-driven. Court-centric. Win-Lose dynamic.

Court is, by its very nature, inherently contentious. After all, you're in a lawsuit! You and your soon-to-be-ex are suing each other. From the outset, you're pursuing an adversarial process where "technically" there's a winner and a loser, but in reality, any sense of triumph or winning by one disputant—or "combatant"—will be short-lived. Even if you get everything you think you want, what you want right now—at the height of negativity—may not be rational or reflective of what is best for your children. Further, while technically it may be correct to view litigation as "win-lose", it's really, "lose-lose-lose," as the emotional destruction and financial costs imposed ensure that you lose, your soon-to-be-ex loses, and most unfortunately, your children lose. The only real winners in a litigated divorce tend to be the attorneys who will happily take your money.

> *"In the adversarial construct, an attorney's job is to advance their client's position - not advance what is in the best interest of the child, which is the role of the judge." - Frank P. Cervone, Esq.*

Let's look at the case of Martin and Mary—a common scenario in a litigated divorce. Martin wants equal timeshare with the kids. Fanatical about the holidays, in the past, Martin decorated the house for Christmas, took the family to his parents' for Thanksgiving and dressed in costume for Halloween. He, therefore, believes that the kids should spend every holiday with him. His rigidity on this issue so enrages Mary that she responds by insisting that she have full custody of the kids. Neither of these positions is realistic, nor are they best for their children. Nonetheless, their attorneys—who are incentivized by billable hours and their "responsibility" to advance their respective client's positions irrespective of children's needs—are more than happy to fight their clients' battle.

After more than a year of fighting back and forth, they end up with a 35-65 shared parenting arrangement, with alternating holidays—a very common outcome. However, they spent a total of $80,000 on attorney fees and costs. For what? It's not an attorney's job or in their financial interest to bring their client down to reality. Moreover, when clients feel as though their attorney isn't advancing their position (no matter how unreasonable as it may be), they tend to replace them with one who will. Ultimately, however, neither Martin nor Mary are happy with the outcome, which they feel was forced upon them. Moreover, Martin will never know whether he might have received a higher timeshare, had he and Mary attempted to resolve their differences by working together, rather than fighting against each other.

Sadly, Martin and Mary's experience is the norm. The litigious path involves many Family Court appearances, or, at least, costly and filing destructive pleadings for court hearings that are ultimately resolved without judicial intervention. At a minimum, it involves extensive law and motion practice through attorneys (or the parties themselves, if self-represented), but can often include judges, custody evaluators, mental health professionals, and other such "experts." Moreover, parents seem incapable or unwilling to view the litigation process from their children's perspective and the impact it has on them.

Does the litigious Family Court model even make sense?

> **"Outcomes are typically determined by the way in which the 'game' is designed." — Mark B. Baer, Esq.**

According to the American Bar Association (ABA), just one out of every 200 family law cases goes to trial—which doesn't mean that generally there aren't plenty of motions filed. However, if fewer than one percent of cases go to trial, how many motions were filed merely because of the way in which the system is designed? More importantly, why is the system designed based on an adversarial paradigm?

In many states, parents are required to attend Conciliation Court before a judge can rule on the case. In California, for example, approximately 70 percent of custody and visitation motions filed are settled through Conciliation Court. Conciliation court is also known as "mandatory mediation" or "court-ordered mediation"; however, as the dynamics are fundamentally different, this form of mediation should not be confused with "true mediation"—a process we'll explain later in this chapter. Mediators in "free mediation" are almost always overworked and inundated in cases; likewise, you have no idea how skilled or effective they are at conflict resolution, or whether they are even passionate about mediation. While conciliation court is "free," there is a significant cost both financially and emotionally in filing a Request for Order with the court to access that "free mediation."

Further, in order to schedule a "mediation" through Conciliation Court in most jurisdictions, you must have a pending hearing—in other words, you must have a child custody or visitation dispute. Because this form of mediation can't take place until after litigation has commenced, both parties have already put their feet in the sand and assumed an adversarial posture. You will now file Motions and Requests for Orders, which tend to contain nasty allegations—often exaggerated, or worse, sometimes fabricated— that can be hurtful and emotionally damaging. You can't take your words back—they become public record heightening bitter feelings and making it that much harder to lessen conflict later. As they say, "the pen is mightier than the sword." So, while Conciliation Court may be technically "free", don't underestimate the potentially significant financial and emotional costs.

> **"The best way to predict the future is to create it."** —
> **Peter Drucker**

Finally, we should also consider, if approximately 70 percent of cases are settled through Conciliation Court, this leaves 30 percent that aren't settled through such means. What portion of the 30 percent could have been resolved without court intervention had the parties attempted to do so before making nasty allegations against each other in pleadings filed with the court? Wouldn't it be better to avoid litigation in the first place, find a mediator that you and your soon-to-be-ex can agree upon, and avoid court altogether?

An attorney's approach can be part of the solution or part of the problem

As we illustrated in the previous section: while Family Court is not inherently evil, the adversarial nature of litigation and court exacerbates conflict and can cause parents and children significant emotional trauma. Don't get us wrong, many attorneys have their hearts in the right place. Likewise, there are many good judges who want to do the right thing. In fact, most judges would prefer you and your soon-to-be-ex resolve your issues and come to agreements outside of court. But the Family Court doesn't lend itself well to resolving conflict or determining family matters. It may be good for deciding criminal matters or business disputes, but court is a terribly unhealthy place to address disputes for people involved in familial and interpersonal relationships.

Now, while many well-intentioned lawyers practice family law, research shows that the legal profession attracts a disturbingly high number of individuals who "thrive" in competitive, adversarial environments that by their nature promote conflict and win-lose outcomes—like family court. Many attorneys possess overly competitive and aggressive personalities that may help them "win" battles, but also inhibit their ability to be peacemakers and problem solvers. Why is this so?

A major contributor is a lack of emotional intelligence. Attorneys tend to be logical, analytical, and rule-oriented people—attributes associated with lower levels of emotional intelligence, including empathy. A November 2014 article published in the American Bar Association's ABA Journal titled, "How to Curb the Law Firm Exodus?", claims not only does law school promote an erosion of empathy, but those with higher levels of sociability and empathy drop out of law school and the legal field at much higher rates than attorneys who lack these critical personality traits.

Equally disturbing, a concerning number of attorneys suffer from psychological issues and substance abuse, yet fear the stigma of seeking help. The American Bar Association estimates 18 to 20 percent of the nation's lawyers abuse alcohol or drugs. Similarly, The Bar Examiner published a survey of 3,300 law students by the University of St. Thomas in Minnesota—"Helping Law Students Get The Help They Need" (Dec 2015). The survey revealed that more than a quarter of law students had received at least one diagnosis of "depression, anxiety, eating disorders, psychosis, personality disorder, and/or substance use disorder." However, only four percent of would-be lawyers said they had ever relied on a health professional to deal with alcohol or drug abuse.

According to Patrick Krill, a former land-use lawyer in Los Angeles, who directs the Legal Professionals Program at the Hazelden Betty Ford Foundation, "There's a widely held belief that lawyers struggle with substance abuse, depression, and anxiety at a very high rate." Jerome Organ, a law professor and one of the authors of the University of St. Thomas in Minnesota's survey, provides a cautionary warning: He states that the effect of untreated addiction or depression in lawyers could affect their ability to serve clients. "If I am dealing with mental health issues that are untreated, and I am not taking care of myself, I'm probably not going to be able to take care of someone else well."

So, why is that these problems seem to be so prevalent in the legal field? In the book, *Daring Greatly,* Brené Brown identifies what she calls the "Viking or Victim" mentality—a win-lose, zero-sum thinking disposition that may "succeed" in court, but often causes difficulties in the real world. Those who possess a "Viking or Victim" mentality—as is common among lawyers—ascribe to a worldview in which one person's win requires another person's loss. These people have difficulty in conceiving of a scenario that is "win-win". Unfortunately, this "win-lose" mentality becomes a self-perpetuating reality.

In her research, Dr. Brown interviewed many attorneys who shared life experiences with recurrent themes of "high-risk behaviors, divorces, disconnection, loneliness, addiction, anger, [and] exhaustion." But, rather than recognizing the negative consequences of behaviors consistent with a Viking-or-Victim worldview, these individuals viewed this as affirming their belief in the brutal win-or-lose reality of life. Brown summarizes:

> Either you are a Victim in life—a sucker or a loser who's always being taken advantage of or can't hold their own–or you're a Viking—someone who sees the threat of being victimized as a constant, so you stay in control, you dominate, you exert your power over things, and you never show vulnerability.

The Viking, who fears falling victim and is obsessed with protecting oneself, will exhibit power by controlling and dominating others; likewise, they see vulnerability as a weakness.

> *"[W]hen we lead, teach, or preach from a gospel of Viking or Victim, win or lose, we crush faith, innovation, creativity, and adaptability to change..."*
> — *Brené Brown*

Dr. Brown points out that people with these personality types are emotionally detached, driven by perfectionism and have an overly aggressive drive to succeed at all costs—their success is predicated on "winning" by defeating an opponent. Sadly, not only can this mentality infect their home lives, but their professional lives and affect those with whom they work. Brown says, "With this lens, there are only two possible positions that people can occupy—power over, or powerless..." The consequences of this mentality are depressing. Brown continues, "Reducing our life options to such limited and extreme roles leaves very little hope for transformation and meaningful change."

Unsurprisingly, the black and white thinking of Viking-Victim, win-or-lose, succeed-or-fail, does not align with what most people would view as "success". According to Brown:

> Survival or winning may be success in the midst of competition, combat, or trauma, but when the immediacy of that threat is removed, merely surviving is not living…. Love and belonging are irreducible needs of men, women, and children, and love and belonging are impossible to experience without vulnerability. Living without connection—without knowing love and belonging—is not victory. Fear and scarcity fuel the Viking-or-Victim approach and part of reintegrating vulnerability means examining shame triggers; what's fueling the win-or-lose fear?

Particularly in the context of divorce, individuals who are predisposed to the Viking-Victim mentality lack the ability to fully appreciate the vulnerability and humanity of those most affected by litigation—parents and children. Is it any surprise that many of the brightest, most compassionate, and altruistic family law attorneys experience burnout and either drop out of traditional family law roles or shift to mediation or collaborative divorce?

On the other end of the spectrum are people who embrace a paradigm of "wholeheartedness." People who adopt this model are more often attracted to professions that promote healing, harmony, and conflict resolution. They embrace cultivating trust and connection in relationships and view these as prerequisites to work harmoniously with people in a manner that encourages cooperation—not combat.

One problem in family law, among others, is that too many attorneys ascribe to the Viking-Victim mentality, and this mentality influences how they define their "professional responsibilities and ethical duties." At a dinner recently, a dentist friend said, "The law, as practiced, is all about winning and not about the truth." This belief is a common perception among the public, and one that's not far from the truth.

On a positive note, however, there are attorneys who practice mediation, collaborative law, and even some who practice traditional family law, whose values do align with characteristics more common on the opposite end of the spectrum; values more closely aligned with "wholeheartedness". These professionals work with a different canvas than those with the Viking-Victim mindset, and predictably, they are far more likely to help you achieve a harmonious outcome that is best—emotionally and financially—for you and your family.

What are the true costs of litigation?

Judge Michael J. Raphael, Michael M. Farhang and Christopher A. Nowlin wrote an article titled, "Just Discovery," published in the November 2015 edition of *Los Angeles Lawyer Magazine* which states:

> "DISCOVERY DISPUTES and motion practice consume a significant portion of the dockets of California Superior Court judges... For many civil judges, a third or more of the motions they hear pertain to discovery disputes, and plaintiffs' and defense attorneys also spend a significant amount of their time and their clients' resources litigating discovery disputes in order to further their positions."

The article documents how ridiculous litigators can be, the juvenile games they play in the name of "litigation tactics," and their inability or unwillingness to negotiate—among other things. Keep in mind what the job of a lawyer is: They are gladiators who are retained to effectuate a "win" for their client. Winning is not about the truth. For that reason, part of an attorney's job involves exploiting the biases held by the judge or members of the jury. Furthermore, they will make every effort to have evidence of the truth excluded if it goes against their client and they can possibly have it excluded through legal technicalities. Decisions in court are **not** based upon the actual facts; rather, they are based upon legally relevant and admissible evidence.

The average cost of a divorce in the United States has long been estimated at $20,000.00 per person or $40,000.00 per couple. However, these figures are misleading, discounting the true costs. They are an average cost of all divorce cases filed, including, but not limited to, those that are fully litigated, negotiated by rival lawyers, and mediated. The cost of fully litigated cases is estimated to cost three times as much as those negotiated by rival lawyers, which cost approximately four times as much as those which are mediated. They also don't include the legal fees and costs incurred post-divorce, which at $250-$500 per hour can add up quickly. Remember, family law cases are considered the vampires of the legal field because of the ongoing legal rematches on any and all issues left open for possible modification for legitimate public policy reasons. Those litigated rematches occur as a result of the win-lose paradigm from which litigation operates, including negotiation by rival lawyers.

> *"While both parents battle each other to try and prove that what they WANT is in the best interest of the child, they spend their child's college tuition, exacerbate the conflict, increase the distrust between them, destroy their ability to effectively co-parent, and harm the child." — Mark Baer, Esq.*

Unfortunately, litigation is the default dispute-resolution process. If, however, as a society we valued harmony and the preservation of family and interpersonal relationships, we would abandon this method as our default process. At least, you have a choice and can opt out of this process—although both parties must agree to do so. Do everything you can to control your emotions, rather than to allow your fear and anger lead you toward litigation.

> *"When parents litigate, the only person involved in the case responsible for assessing what's in the child's best interest is the judge. However, a judge's knowledge of the family is so limited, too often their subjective determination may not actually be in the best interest of the child." — Mark Baer, Esq.*

Beyond the fact that litigation is emotionally and financially costly, it is a destructive method to try to resolve disputes because it's about blame, rather than personal responsibility. Its very nature runs contrary to the acceptance of one's own contribution to the situation while it tends to do nothing to resolve any problems that led to the dispute in the first place.

As Warren Berger, then Chief Justice of the United States Supreme Court, said, "Our system is too costly, too painful, too destructive, too inefficient for a truly civilized people. To rely on the adversary process as the principal means of resolving conflicting claims is a mistake that must be corrected."

In the event you feel compelled to choose litigation, choose counsel wisely. It's far more about their personality and philosophy than their hourly rate. How litigation oriented (court-centric) are they? Are they well-reputed for escalating or de-escalating the level of conflict? Of course, instead of choosing to go down the destructive path of litigation, wouldn't it be better to agree with your spouse from the outset to resolve your divorce through one of the cooperative methods outlined below?

Cooperative Divorce

Mediation or Collaborative divorce. Solution-focused. Child-centric. Lower cost. Faster. Win-Win dynamic.

By now, you're likely convinced that Family Court is the last place you want to be! Fortunately, you can avoid court. While ultimately a judge will have to sign off on your divorce, if you choose one of the cooperative models described below, you can stay out of court saving your family a lot of money and heartache.

Unlike the adversarial approach to family law, mediation and collaborative law are solution-oriented. When divorcing, people often confuse their legal rights and positions with their personal values. This is why in true mediation or collaborative divorce, professionals employ what is known as "interest-based negotiation"—also known as "integrative bargaining" or "win-win negotiation". Interest-based negotiation is a strategy which considers the underlying causes of problems and helps find solutions that best suit the parties' unique needs and interests.

Depending on your situation, in a cooperative divorce, you may (or may not) enlist more professionals than in a combative, litigated divorce. However, the fundamental difference is that if you hire the right professionals (who possess the right personality, philosophy, and skill set), and believe in the process, these professionals will take a reconciliatory—and sometimes even a therapeutic—approach, rather than an adversarial one. Ultimately, you will expend far less financial and emotional resources than heading down that dark hole called "litigation."

In a cooperative divorce—whether you choose mediation or collaboration—you and your soon-to-be-ex determine the approach best for your family. Both mediation and collaborative law were designed to help you to end your marriage and resolve your issues in a constructive manner.

Mediation

Mediation varies based on both style and design. When we refer to mediation in this chapter, we are referring to "facilitative mediation," which is the original form of mediation. In this model, the mediator sets up and maintains a safe and comfortable environment within which to assist the parties in resolving their dispute. The mediator maintains an atmosphere of mutual respect and helps the parties communicate with each other. The mediator also helps the parties uncover the reasons underlying their respective positions, to flesh out their actual needs and interests.

Once this information comes to light, the mediator encourages creative problem solving to resolve or otherwise manage the conflict, while still satisfying the needs and interests of each party. The parties may retain consulting attorneys (ideally, mediation-minded attorneys) and jointly retain experts to provide information they deem helpful or otherwise necessary to reach an agreement. The mediator may assist the parties in evaluating the feasibility of various potential solutions. Reaching a mutually satisfying resolution is the goal of facilitative mediation.

Collaborative Divorce

The collaborative model may provide you with more opportunities to tailor plans to your family's unique needs because it incorporates all of the skills needed to increase the likelihood of a successful outcome through its interdisciplinary team approach. You need not navigate litigation system since going to court is not an option. No spouse is allowed to go to court during the collaborative divorce process. Therefore, it is a process free from threats of litigation. Each party has an attorney to ensure that any power imbalance is taken out of the process. However, unlike in litigation, the attorneys for each party are treated as vital parts of the settlement team, not adversaries. Furthermore, parenting decisions put the interests of the children first. This model could not be more different from litigation.

Additionally, both mediation and collaborative divorce tend to be less stressful not only for you and your ex, but your family and friends as well. Both processes promote communication and cooperation. Rather than finger-pointing to assess blame and fault, as is done in litigation, these processes are future-focused, thereby enabling parties to solve problems. In fact, such a solution-focused approach allows the parties to reach agreements and accomplish things of importance to them that may be beyond the scope of what a judge can legally do.

These processes are also designed to reduce the conflict between the parties, which benefits them and their children. In so doing, these approaches help people to heal faster and create a healthier future for themselves and their children. As an added benefit, the research shows that people tend to comply with obligations reached on their own through cooperation, than with those imposed by court order or through "coercive" means. As if that's not enough, they are confidential processes, unlike court cases, which are matters of public record.

Benefits of a Cooperative Divorce

Let's summarize the benefits of a cooperative divorce:

- **It is non-adversarial:** Resolving issues through communication and working as a team, instead of fighting against each other (whether in court or otherwise); mediators and collaborative law professionals help parties focus on a mutually satisfactory outcome.

- **It's a creative & open process:** Avoid the adversarial "win at all costs" positioning of attorneys who cannot offer solutions due to strategic reasons; instead, professionals can freely offer solutions from a perspective that appreciates both parties' needs.

- **Save money...Lots of money:** Hold on to your money for your family rather than funding the college fund for your attorney's children. You pay only for the number of meetings you need to reach an agreement, rather than drafting motions and spending endless hours preparing for and battling in court. It's not uncommon for families to be left in financial ruin after a litigated divorce. Don't make this mistake.

- **Save time:** Resolution usually comes much faster, sometimes within just a few sessions. You and your soon-to-be-ex establish the timeframe to resolve issues; you don't have to wait months to get a new court date. Instead, you work as a team.

- **Reduce stress & anxiety:** Conflict and living with unresolved issues for a prolonged period of time can be stressful. Because cooperative processes save time, money and reduce conflict, you'll have to live with far less stress than that which is present in a litigated divorce.

- **Enjoy more flexibility:** Professionals are far more flexible, often available to work evenings or weekends around your schedule. In court, on the other hand, you're dependent on the court's busy schedule, often waiting months to see a judge on a single issue.

- **Preserve confidentiality:** Your meetings are private and all of your documents and communications not filed with the court are considered privileged information. By contrast, in court, you argue your case publicly before a judge and others, and your court file typically becomes a public record. Can you imagine sharing highly personal and private issues with strangers?

- **Receive personal attention**: Most family courts are overburdened and understaffed; judges are overworked with a great number of cases. In true mediation and collaborative divorce, you work as a team to develop more potential solutions and gain consensus.

- **Improve post-divorce compliance & stability:** You will co-parent (and be a co-parent) with your soon-to-be ex for years. That doesn't end when your children turn 18. Cooperative processes help facilitate effective communication while minimizing conflict. Likewise, you may re-engage the same professionals should a conflict later emerge.

- **Maintain control:** The cooperative processes are voluntary and, as parents, you control what you want to discuss while working together to determine the outcome of your case. In Family Court, on the other hand, you cede control to a judge to decide what they believe is best for your family. You always have time to think about proposed agreements, and you decide if what is proposed works for you. Who understands your family's needs better? You or a judge?

- **Preserve civil communication channels with your ex:** Maintain channels of civil communication, rather than using attorneys to act as your proxy.

- **Focus on your children and insulate them from conflict:** Cooperative processes protect your children. If you go to court, your children may be required to be interviewed or observed by various "experts." Your children may even be compelled to appear before the court. This experience subjects your children to elevated conflict, tension, anxiety, loyalty conflicts, etc. The long-term damage to your children can be severe. However, in cooperative processes, the right professionals will help you and your soon-to-be-ex maintain focus on your children's needs.

Can I use mediation or collaborative law if my soon-to-be-ex has a personality disorder, high-conflict personality, or is controlling?

The better question may be, "Can I afford not to attempt to use mediation or collaborative law if my soon-to-be-ex has a personality disorder, high-conflict personality, or is controlling?" According to Bill Eddy, LCSW, Esq. Co-Founder and President of the High Conflict Institute, "in high-conflict divorce, one or both parties in many— if not most—have an unrecognized mental health issue or personality disorder characterized by a refusal to accept personal responsibility for one's actions, blaming others and denial." As Eddy points out, unfortunately, family lawyers, judges and other professionals are not trained to identify these issues, nor are they well equipped to deal with them:

Sadly, Family Courts provide a forum for people with such problems today (in contrast to when I began practicing law), especially because family lawyers, judges and other professionals are not trained in identifying mental health issues, get stuck arguing about them out of ignorance and there are few mental health resources for treating them even if they were properly identified. Family courts were never designed to diagnose and treat mental health issues, and the adversarial process is guaranteed to fail at it. Reforms need to involve more mental health training for professionals and more conflict resolution skills for clients to help them make decisions out of court in non-adversarial settings."

While many professionals are of the opinion that high-conflict cases can't be handled through mediation or collaborative law, Eddy, who is recognized as the leading expert in high-conflict divorce, disagrees. Eddy believes that by working with professionals who have the right skill set and approach, as many as 90% of cases involving individuals with personality disorders (or high conflict personalities) can be successfully resolved through mediation.

For the process to be successful Eddy identifies crucial elements for a high-conflict mediation:

- **Structure and focus**—Psychologists have long recognized both are crucial when working with individuals with personality disorders

- **Modeling**—The mediator should model the behavior they would like imitated—it is well-recognized within the psychological community that individuals learn new behavior through conscious or unconscious imitation

- **Connection**—The mediator should connect with those in conflict with attention, empathy and respect

- **Consequences**—The mediator should educate participants on what potential consequences their choices may elicit

When a skilled mediator employs all of these concepts, Eddy claims the likelihood of success increases significantly. (A valuable resource to learn more is Bill Eddy's High Conflict Institute www.highconflictinstitute.com. Mr. Eddy has also authored many of the most popular books on dealing with high-conflict personalities.)

Overall, litigation is unlikely to elicit a better result or end up being a better alternative to cooperative processes. While some cases will require litigation, it really should be used as means of last resort.

Michele Lowrance, author of The Good Karma Divorce and a former Family Court judge was once skeptical about the use of mediation or collaborative law for high conflict cases, but ultimately became an enthusiastic proponent:

> If I did not have firsthand experience in successfully mediating high-conflict cases, I might still believe that difficult divorce cases require a judge to make the final decisions...Mediation presents a better alternative to litigation for high-conflict and high-asset cases because it offers a non-adversarial setting...Each time you go to court to solve a problem, you further polarize the parties and their chances of settling become progressively smaller.

Final Considerations: How to Hire the 'Right' Mediation or Collaborative Divorce Team

By now, you should have a clear understanding of why taking a cooperative approach to your divorce is typically far better than a combative approach. In general, both collaborative law and mediation are vastly superior options to litigation. However, know that not all mediation processes or the mediators who facilitate them are equal. Likewise, not all collaborative law processes or collaborative law practitioners are the same.

Take note that simply because someone calls themselves a mediator or collaborative law practitioner does not mean they possess the right personality, philosophy and skill set, or that they believe in the process. For example, a court may mandate mediation, but court-ordered mediation may be facilitated by someone who does not have extensive training in mediation or conflict resolution. Likewise, former judges who call themselves "mediators" generally do not provide real mediation; rather, they assess your case and advise you on what they **believe** the "likely outcome" will be should you choose to go to court.

According to Stephen Willis, Ph.D., an expert on the subject of collaboration, "People who only focus on the structure or mechanics of the collaboration process can more readily get stuck, taken advantage of, and end up with collaboration failure, possibly on a historic grand scale."

He describes the following five different personality types:

1. Collaborator

2. Cooperator

3. Competitor

4. Enslaver

5. Predator

Collaborative potential is a function of both the personality type and motivation for cooperation. Because professionals are not part of your family, they don't have the same motivating factors that exist for parents who share a bond through their children. Most parents share values, mission, family ties, and common goals (as discussed in chapter one). Therefore, the personality type of any professionals you work with must be higher on the collaborative scale.

Unsurprisingly, attorneys tend to fall in the Competitor category or even further down on that scale, underscoring the importance of finding a professional (or professionals) who are "true" mediators or collaborative divorce practitioners, and conform to the Collaborator or Cooperator personality types. It's also important to note that individuals who conform to the Collaborator personality type find satisfaction in the successes of others.

According to Dr. Willis, "The predisposition and aspiration to collaborate are 'strong' for Collaborators, 'modest' for Cooperators, 'weak' for Competitors, 'negligible' for Enslavers, and 'none' for Predators." Dr. Willis explains that collaboration naturally works best when dealing with Collaborators and Cooperators. Collaboration becomes increasingly more difficult and potentially dangerous, depending where on this scale the personality types involved range. One's chances to achieve a successful collaboration are greatly increased the higher up the scale all participants in the process place—professionals and parents alike.

In your search, reach out to a few different professionals and get a better sense of their background and experience.

Ten Questions to Ask a Potential Mediator or Collaborative Divorce Attorney

The following are some of the questions to ask to help determine who to retain as a family law mediator or collaborative law practitioner:

1. Have you personally been involved in a divorce? If so, was it handled through negotiation, mediation, collaborative divorce or litigation? Reflecting back on it now, what, if anything, would you have done differently?

2. Is there a way of proceeding that would both allow me to protect my interests and minimize the amount of hurt to everyone, including my spouse?

3. Can you assist me in determining which issues are worth pursuing, and which are not?

4. How can we effectively proceed in the easiest and quickest possible way?

5. How do you define a successful outcome?

6. Other than acting as mediator or collaborative divorce practitioner, what is your background with regard to family law?

7. How much experience do you have mediating family law matters or working as a collaborative practitioner?

8. What is your perspective with regard to the involvement of attorneys in the mediation process?

9. What other types of professionals do you work with in the mediation process, if any, and why?

10. What formal mediation and/or collaborative law training, if any, have you received?

And, finally, follow your instincts. Do they seem compassionate and empathetic? Are they passionate about what they do?

Mediators and collaborative divorce professionals can do wonders to help you through your divorce, but, ultimately, it requires that both parties be willing to work with each other to reach agreements and move beyond entrenched positions, rather than fighting against each other. As you approach the mediation and collaborative divorce process, be sure to keep an open mind and be willing to work through your emotions for the greater good. While a divorce is never an easy journey, if you maintain positivity, resilience, and a willingness to choose cooperation over combat, you'll be happier — and so will your kids!

For further resources and to listen to DivorceBuddy.co podcasts, visit DivorceBuddy.co.

To learn more about California's "Most Compassionate Mediator," Mark Baer, Esq., visit his website MarkBaerEsq.com or read his Huffington Post Blog. For further reading, visit:

- The Perfect Storm: Lawyer Limitations and the Adversarial Model in Family Law

- What Is Required to Make Collaborative Divorce Truly Collaborative?

- How to Select the Best Mediator Is a Must Read for Everyone

References:

Brown, Brené. *Daring Greatly: How the Courage to Be Vulnerable Transforms the Way We Live, Love, Parent, and Lead*. Avery Group, 2015. Print.

Eddy, Bill A. *High Conflict People in Legal Disputes*. High Conflict Institute, 2012. Print.

Eddy, William A., and Randi Kreger. *Splitting: Protecting Yourself While Divorcing Someone with Borderline or Narcissistic Personality Disorder*. Oakland, CA: New Harbinger Publications, 2011. Print.

Lowrance, Michele. *The Good Karma Divorce: Avoid Litigation, Turn Negative Emotions into Positive Actions, and Get on with the Rest of Your Life*. New York, NY: Harper One, 2010. Print.

Organ, Jerome M., David B. Jaffe, and Katherine M. Bender. "Helping Law Students Get The Help They Need: An Analysis of Data Regarding Law Students' Reluctance to Seek Help." *The Bar Examiner*. National Conference of Bar Examiners, Dec. 2015. Web. 02 Feb. 2016.

Raphael, Judge Michael, Michael M. Farhang, and Christopher A. Nowlin. "Just Discovery." *Los Angeles County Bar Association - Los Angeles Lawyer Magazine* (2015). Web.

Scott, Todd C. "Law Trends & News: Managing Lawyer Treatment." *American Bar Association.* Spring 2011. 02 Feb. 2016. Web.

Weiss, Debra Cassens. "How to Curb the Law Firm Exodus? Study Looks at Traits of Those Most Likely to Leave Law Practice." *ABA Journal.* American Bar Association. 02 Jan. 2016. Web.

Willis, Dr. Stephen. *Power Through Collaboration: The Formula for Success in Challenging Situations.* Willis Consulting (www.PowerThroughCollaboration.com), 2013. Print.

ABOUT MARK B. BAER, ESQ

Recognized by the National Association of Distinguished Counsel in an elite class of the nation's top one percent of attorneys, Mark Baer, mediator, collaborative divorce practitioner, author, lecturer, keynote speaker and legal analyst, is one of the most accomplished professionals in family law. A former family law litigator, Mark witnessed firsthand the inherent flaws of the family court system. Recognizing mediation as a far less destructive approach to divorce than family court, Mark left litigation in 2012, and has not been back to court since. A thought leader in many areas of family law, Mark is recognized for his provocative and forward-thinking ideas on improving the way in which family law is handled.

Mark is a frequent contributor to both the San Gabriel Valley Psychological Association's newsletter and the popular, Huffington Post. His articles have also appeared in the American Journal of Family Law, Los Angeles Daily Journal, MariaShriver.com, and many other respected publications. Mark was also a contributing author in the book, "Inside the Minds: Strategies for Family Law in California", published by Thomson Reuters in 2013.

Mr. Baer has presented at many conferences, including the American Bar Association's Section of Family Law Conference and the California Psychological Association (CPA) Convention. Mark is also a Wevorce Associate, Attorney & Mediator at Wevorce and a co-founder of Family Dynamics Assistance Center.

In 2015, Corporate America magazine selected Mark as the "Most Compassionate Family Mediator – California" for the 2015 Legal Elite Awards. Mark studied business economics at UCLA, and earned his law degree from Loyola Law School, Los Angeles.

To learn more about Mark, visit www.markbaeresq.com. Follow his column on Huffington Post at http://www.huffingtonpost.com/mark-baer/.

CHAPTER THREE

For Kids - What Divorce Breaks Apart, Strong Co-Parenting Rebuilds

by Karen Bonnell

> *"Separation/divorce is the end of an intimate partnership for adults, not the end of a family for children." — Karen Bonnell*

When we embarked on this project, one of the first people who came to mind was best-selling author and relationship coach, Karen Bonnell. I absolutely wanted Karen to participate, because I knew she would be perfect for this book. With over 30 years of experience working with individuals, couples, and families facing transition, loss, stress and change, Karen embodies the mission of this book—putting kids first.

As a co-parenting coach and author of "The Co-Parents' Handbook: Raising Well-Adjusted, Resilient, and Resourceful Kids in a Two-Home Family from Little Ones to Young Adults," Karen has observed that while conflict comes with the territory, loving parents have an opportunity to do what's best for their children. Every parent has the capacity—and as long as they have the desire—they can commit themselves to develop their co-parenting skills and put aside ill feelings towards their ex in order to put their children first and raise their children to grow into happy and emotionally healthy adults.

In this interview, and through her life's work, Karen stresses how important it is for parents to work together and use family court only as a last resort. Family court is court; it's a place that is by nature, win-lose and adversarial, so anything you can do as a parent to stay out of court will be a positive force financially and emotionally—and everyone will be better off for it.

Flexibility, compromise, cooperation. These are recurrent themes through Karen's work. Karen's approach has been proven and tested to help parents confidently take on the challenges of raising children in two homes.

During the course of the conversation, Karen addresses many of the most common issues parents face during divorce:

- The importance of creating a parenting plan collaboratively rather than relying on the court

- How to create a roadmap for all members of the family to safely navigate through separation, divorce, and beyond

- How to effectively communicate with your ex in a manner that minimizes conflict and misunderstanding

- How to communicate with your children about the divorce and support them emotionally through their family change

- How to avoid the common mistakes and pitfalls parents often encounter when it comes to co-parenting, planning, decision-making, and conflict management

- How to ensure your children feel loved and secure during and after your divorce

Meet Karen

Jeremy: Hi Karen. Can you share with us a little bit about your background and what inspired you to make it your mission to help parents, co-parent more effectively?

Karen: I was part of creating a two-home family myself, for my children and their father before I had any idea about co-parent coaching or divorce coaching in any way, shape, or form. So, like many parents, I went to a divorce attorney, conflict escalated, and I learned a lot about what that process looks like and in retrospect, what was missing. Of course, we found our way through that difficult, emotional terrain, but I came out of that really wanting things to be different for other families.

You wrote what many people consider the "bible" of co-parenting books—the best-selling, "The Co-Parents' Handbook". What inspired you to write it?

"The Co-Parents' Handbook" is the culmination of the teaching practices and the protocols that came out of the last nine years of co-parent coaching in the Collaborative Law Community. I serve as a divorce and co-parent coach. I work with parents to manage strong emotions, to care for their children through their family change, and to construct a skillful parenting plan.

Walking to my office to meet a couple back in 2013, I said to myself, "I should just write this down. There is no reason why people should have to walk into my office to get this information." That's how the book got started; it launched in fall 2014. It is chock full of practical, how-to advice—the skills necessary to co-parent, stay child-centered, and create a secure two-home family.

How to Get Co-Parenting Right

How important is it that parents get their parenting plan right?

Skillfully building a parenting plan is the very first step to building your co-parenting relationship. If you rely on the state and the courts, you're going to get a wider play, a standardized parenting plan that may or may not meet the unique needs of your children, your circumstances or your family.

I really encourage parents that when you approach the parenting planning process, remember that you are the two best people to make these decisions about your children.

Learning to work together, to effectively co-parent, is a life-long gift to them because you will be there at high school graduation. You two will be there, God-willing, for a wedding, a baby naming—all the lifecycle events that are yet to come. They will want you there, stress-free and focused on their joy.

> *"If you rely on the state and the courts, you're going to get a wider play, standardized parenting plan that may or may not meet the unique needs of your children, your circumstances or your family ... remember that you are the two best people to make these decisions about your children."*

In your work, you use the term "uncoupling". What does that mean and how does it impact co-parenting?

Most of the issues between co-parents are actually a result of unresolved marital strife or intimate partner strife. In other words, when we came together, we came together up here, what we would call our "marriage," our "intimate partnership," and from that, we had children, and we became parents. Ending our intimate partnership doesn't change parents' love for their children.

As parents, we want to love and care for our kids; we want what's best for them. I help parents recognize that up here, we're going to uncouple that intimate partnership. This is your spouse-mind. This is the place where you hear, "I hate you. You betrayed me. I don't want anything to do with you." I can't stand your face." That's happening up here.

Down here, on a parent level, because we want what's best for our children, we hear, "You're my kid's dad. You're my kid's mom. I want them to be healthy. For that reason and that reason alone, I am going to co-parent with you in the best way possible. I want that future for our children."

Avoid Common Mistakes

During a divorce, there are a lot of challenges. What would you say are the common mistakes and pitfalls parents make when it comes to co-parenting, planning, communicating, and managing conflict?

During a divorce, conflict is high, emotions are high, and too often, it's easy to lose our heads. That dinosaur brain, when it gets activated, that tail is swinging around and creating all kinds of damage. Triggered, emotionally flooded, saying and doing things we'd never do under different circumstances. As much as I can, I try to help parents recognize that probably the single most destructive element in a divorce process for children is what can become chronic, toxic conflict.

Now, I'm not talking about healthy conflict. I'm not even talking about disagreements that I might have with you. I'm talking about the things I say and do, and often, with and to my children, that are intended to hurt you. Using our children, getting them caught in the middle, saying ugly things about you when I know that half of their heart belongs to you, right? They love and care about us both, and I need to protect that, so managing my emotions and that toxic conflict is real important.

Another issue is when we compete. Somehow believing that what's best for kids is what I have to deliver as a parent, not what you have to deliver. We have to find our way to a place where we are both able to parent our children, so they can receive what's best about both of us. I like to say, "What's best for kids is two healthy, capable, engaged parents."

> *"What's best for kids is two healthy, capable, engaged parents."*

How to Communicate with Your Children

We know that with children, we need to be sensitive about how we communicate certain things; when and what should we tell our kids about the separation?

When and what to tell your children about the decision to become a two-home family has much to do with their ages. Younger children—under age 8—do better with less than seven to ten day's lead time telling them something is going to change and the beginning of the change. The change doesn't have to be abrupt. The more you think through the transition and ensure it's well paced, the smoother it will be for the kids.

Older children can understand that you've made a decision and it will take a bit longer to implement.

Older children benefit from watching you work together as parents for as long as a month or more prior to one of you actually moving out or making a similar change in the structure of the family. The important issue here is that they are clear that you have made a final decision, that you're taking steps forward, and that they have no role in reversing the course of this important family change.

The key is your ability to work together as parents: managing conflict, solving problems, sharing childcare duties in a planned way, while taking steps to transition the family to a new structure.

Remember: you are changing your adult relationship, ending an intimate partnership. Your children aren't a part of that highly personal adult relationship—and have limited ability to understand intimate partnership—even teens. Although your intimate partnership is completing or ending, parents and children don't divorce. You are building a new co-parenting relationship—and yet there is nothing new about being parents to your children.

What is new, is how you will share them throughout the days, weeks and years ahead and how you integrate their lives across two homes. Your co-parenting relationship directly affects your children and what matters most to them. "Who will tuck me in and read stories?" "Who will help me with my homework?" "Who will take me to driver's ed?"

Hold dearly this Co-Parents' Credo: *I will not let the mistakes and the failures of my marriage become the mistakes and the failures of my co-parenting relationship. This I commit to my co-parent and to my children.*

(Note: For a brief video on "How to Tell Your Children About Divorce/ Separation," please go to www.thecoparentshandbook.com*).*

There are circumstances in some situations—for example, an affair— that may have caused considerable strife and hurt in our relationship. Clearly, this is an area where we want to tread lightly and insulate our children, yet we also don't want to lie. When we communicate with our children about the divorce, how do we best handle these types of situations?

That's a really good question. I have not met a parent today who wants to lie to their children, and this can be a really tricky circumstance. As much as children need to understand what's happening with their family, they need age-appropriate, accurate information. They don't necessarily need the truth about our intimate partnership. One of the things I joke with parents about is, if your kids walked in one day, you know, back when you were a one-home family and said, "So, do you and dad have oral sex?" you probably would say, "Uh, that's none of your business." Right?

It's not the first place you're going to go to give all the truth about your sex life. Why would we do that now about what's going on in our intimate partnership?

This isn't about parenting. This is about adults. Let's keep adult information on the adult level, so that when we want to provide parenting information like: How is this family changing, how are mom and dad, or mom and mom, or dad and dad, going to take care of you? Kids need that information, and they need it to be accurate.

Now, caveat there. You don't always know the answer. So, I encourage parents to say in those moments when they don't know: "Are we going to keep our house?"

"Sweetie, you know what? Mom and I haven't figured that out." or,

"Dad and I don't know that yet, but as soon as we know, we'll let you know. What you can be sure of, is there will be a home with each of us, and you will be well cared for."

We break things down for kids into categories of what we know, what we don't know, what will change, what will not change. "…and what will not change is that we will always be your parents."

There are other things, too, that come up, and I imagine we tread on those differently. For example, let's say we have a new romantic partner. How do we introduce our new partner to our children?

We consider those changes—I put those in a category of a significant change. So, we're going through a separation and divorce. In an ideal world, Jeremy, we're going to stabilize those two homes first, whatever those residences look like. We're going to stabilize our rhythms, we're going to find our way into a schedule, kids are going to feel safe and secure again. Now, that's in an ideal world. We don't always have that luxury because love doesn't happen according to legal documents. It just doesn't. Each parent may have someone or one parent may, so what we want to do is remember we want kids to feel secure. When we introduce a new adult, children feel destabilized again. Not necessarily in a bad way, but we want to recognize that it destabilizes and act accordingly, so we pace the introduction, the amount of time spent together—we stay focused on the kids' needs.

Ideally, this person did not suddenly start spending every weekend with our children and us; they're not moving in yet. Let's talk about how to allow children to develop a relationship—like any relationship with a coach, a teacher, the next-door neighbor, our best friend's parents. Give it some time to mature, so that when it's time for us to become domestic partners, our children aren't destabilized, but rather, they are ready to accept a new person into their lives. Healthy pacing also allows our co-parent, by the way, to feel respected, because one of the frightening things for a co-parent early on when we bring a new person into our lives is, "Does that person think they're going to be my kid's other parent? Whoa, just stop the train because I'm the mom (or I'm the dad)."

There's never any doubt about who are the primary parents, so when a new romantic partner comes into the family system that is separating, new partners need to respect their place. You're not a parent in lieu. You are the partner of one of the parents. Mom and dad are the two adults, the two parents. Those two original parents will always be the co-parent executive officers. Nobody disrupts that. They're the decision makers for those children. I might have a partner; you might have a partner. They're part of our team, but they're not part of the executive team for our kids unless we all agree.

> *Mom and dad are the two adults, the two parents. Those two original parents will always be the co-parent executive officers. Nobody disrupts that.*

You make some really good points, Karen. Sometimes, predictably, one parent may feel jealous if there's a new romantic partner who's been introduced into their children's lives. If you're the parent with the new partner, and you learn that the other parent is disparaging your new romantic partner, do you have any suggestions of how to deal with that?

That's a great time to ask for a meeting with a co-parent coach to talk through how to handle those upset feelings, those competitive feelings, those feelings of being upstaged.

And what about in a situation where perhaps the new romantic partner is misstepping?

Often, when I get co-parents in the office, we have a conversation and we find out that the new—let's just use "girlfriend"—the new girlfriend is putting makeup on our 6-year-old daughter, or buying our 8-year-old skinny jeans, or doing all kinds of cutesy, fun, adult female to younger female things. The mom, who has been responsible for holding boundaries and teaching values is thinking, "Wait a second, I never agreed she could have skinny jeans, and you know what? Makeup is off limits." Those are missteps.

When it comes to "parental intimate behaviors with children," our new romantic partner shouldn't be doing them. It may be fun, but it's a misstep, and so just respecting these boundaries can be really helpful to decrease feelings of competition, jealousy, and violation.

Divorce Does Not Have to Be Destructive

Many people would contend that divorce is always a destructive process on children. Would you agree with that? And, what can parents do to create the best, healthiest outcome for their children? What do kids really need most?

Great question. Divorce, in its pure definition, is a family change—and it is a significant one. Like any significant change in a child's life, it has implications. There's going to be grief. There's going to be anger, upset, fear, and worry. There's going to be a temporary loss of security. As long as we understand that our children are grieving and trying to find their way back into security, we can direct our goals so that we support them emotionally, and repair their sense of loss, and restore that stability and security. Then, while the divorce is a significant family change, it doesn't need to be destructive. It doesn't need to be damaging. If we remain good parents, demonstrate our unconditional love and support for our children, manage conflict appropriately and provide positive, inspiring modeling through the change, divorce doesn't need to disadvantage our children.

These are the key issues, so what we explain to children is, "We're changing from a one-home to a two-home family. Your sense of family is going to include two homes. You're going to have a home with mom and a home with dad. We will take good care of you - you don't need to worry about that."

That's slightly different language than, "Mom's house," "Dad's house," isn't it? Because back in the day, when we'd say, "Mom's house" or "Dad's house," children had no home. It's as if, "I was either at your house or your house, but where is my house?"

Now, we say, "Home with mom and home with dad. Your sense of home goes across two residences, and you're going to be loved and cared for in both."

In that context, we're going to keep our conflict at a minimum. We're not going to let kids get caught in the middle. We're not going to bad mouth and disparage the other parent. We're going to help our family members, and the members of our community, understand that even though they may think they're supporting us [by badmouthing the other parent], this behavior hurts our children. "I don't need it. Please don't support me in that way."

We also need to remember that kids need a strong and engaged relationship with both parents. I'm not going to compete with you and assume that you should just be an every other weekend hamburger-night parent because, after all, I've been home with these kids ever since they were born. No. There are many different parenting schedules that reflect the needs and interests of all members of the family and the unique circumstances of our jobs and children's lives. Working together to respect how best to maintain our work, how to maximize parent-time for our children, and how to build parenting skills where needed to ensure that both parents provide not just financially, but emotionally in that "hands on" loving wat for their children. It's not longer uncommon, that children may go home from school to a home where one parents can be available, while the residential parent swings by after work to pick up the kids to begin his/her residential time. Be international. Respect each other. Know your kids will benefit from an enduring, loving relationship with both of you.

What does a shared relationship look like? It looks like enough time with each parent to have that sense of home, so that they're not visiting with the parent. A parent cares for us. We don't visit with a parent. We visit with an aunt, but we don't visit with a parent. A fully engaged relationship with each parent is what we're after.

> *"What does a shared relationship look like? It looks like enough time with each parent to have that sense of home, so that they're not visiting with the parent.*
>
> *A parent cares for us. We don't visit with a parent. We visit with an aunt, but we don't visit with a parent. A fully engaged relationship with each parent is what we're after."*

Co-Parent with Compassion and Empathy

You mentioned in one of our previous conversations that sometimes parents get caught up in the letter of the law or the agreement, rather than being empathetic and allowing some flexibility under appropriate circumstances. In fact, by being flexible—within reason—we putting our kids first. Could you expound?

When we have a healthy co-parenting relationship, it's going to be easy to go to each other and say, "Hey, I've got a work conference this weekend. I can't get out of it. It's my residential schedule. Would you like to have the kids, or would you care for the kids for me?" Now, I'm not going to assume that you're available. You might not be, but I want the kids to be with you if they can't be with me. That kind of flexibility, that kind of generosity, is normal when we're parenting well together. We still strive for that in a two-home family, just as we would in a one-home family.

If you and I are not getting along and can't communicate, Jeremy, and we're co-parents, we're going to follow that co-parenting plan, that parenting plan as much as possible in order to diminish conflict. That's its value. A well-written, well-crafted parenting plan helps us when the wheels are off the bus. Because, then, I know exactly what to do on Saturday when I have to be at that work conference—I need to make sure the kids are cared for. Now, what you're doing—whether you'll take the kids for me—is irrelevant. I don't have to worry about it, and you aren't going to feel intruded on by me. All those other negative connotations that can come up can be dealt with by following our plan.

We look at, "What is the quality of our co-parenting relationship?" Whether we're friends or not, guess what? Friendship is not required for a strong and skillful co-parenting relationship. It's stability. It's respect. It's healthy boundaries. It's strong communication skills. It's the ability to problem solve. That's what we want in a co-parenting relationship.

> *Friendship is not required for a strong and skillful co-parenting relationship. It's stability. It's respect. It's healthy boundaries. It's strong communication skills. It's the ability to problem solve. That's what we want in a co-parenting relationship.*

If you and I become friends through that process over time again, hallelujah, praise God, that's easy. But if we don't, it doesn't matter. Right? We can still throw a beautiful wedding even if we're not friends—if we can do those other things with enough respect.

Right, those are some great points. Whether there's a friendship there or not, if parents can maintain mutual respect for each other, this will have a huge impact on what's most important. Ultimately, children want to feel secure, correct?

Correct, and our problems are going to get solved, and my activities are going to move forward. "Now, you're going to show up at my soccer game because…guess what? I want you both on the sidelines of my soccer game." That's one of the most important things. "When I look up from blowing out my birthday candles, I see you both there. You don't have to be standing next to each other. Just please both be there.

It's in those moments, my tank is filled, and my heart is filled with the fact that I'm still the most important person to you. And whatever is going on between the two of you is not going to disrupt my getting to have you both."

A couple terms that you use a lot are a "spouse mind" and "parent mind." What do those terms mean exactly?

Let's go back to the uncoupling process for a moment. When I'm having those rageful thoughts or I want to disparage you, because I feel like you've done things that are deceitful, untrustworthy, betraying, and I actually think you've ruined our family, that's in my "spouse-mind". That is how I see it as an intimate partner or as an adult who had hopes and dreams that your decision to leave our relationship has changed. Okay?

That's "spouse mind", but in "parent-mind", I'm thinking to myself, "My kids are so lucky. You are an incredible dad. I know they need you, and I want them to have the experiences and the influences that you have to offer." That's "parent-mind". Learning to discern between the two is really helpful to guide our actions, parenting planning, and our co-parenting relationship.

*Learning to discern between the two is really helpful
to guide our actions, parenting planning, and our co-
parenting relationship.*

**The term "children's best interest" is thrown around a lot in family
court. In legalese, the term is ambiguous, so in the context of parenting,
how do parents figure what is in the best interest of their children?**

Let's go back to the model that we've used when we were married. We
would pay attention: What makes our children unique? What's their
temperament? What are their needs? How do they handle the transition?
What kind of homework support do they need? How much sleep do
they need? What skills do we want our children to build, so that they get
launched into a healthy adulthood? Right?

We're going to look at "what's in their best interest" through that lens.
We're going to ask ourselves the question, "How best can the two of us
together, in separate homes, together, but apart, make sure that those skills,
that those experiences, and that love and security is best maintained?"

The other thing we're going to look at is their development. "Where are
our kids developmentally?" What an infant needs and what a three-year-
old needs will be different from what a 12-year-old needs. We may have
different capacities to provide those needs. While considering circumstances
and availability to parent, we need to match (or build) our parenting skills
by sustaining a strong and engaged relationship with our children and
provide to their needs.

Parents acknowledge their strengths and weaknesses and either build
capacities/skills or allow one of us to meet those needs because that makes
the most sense. What we might do for a 3-year-old can look different when
that child reaches age seven, right? We have all of those ways of looking at

what's best for kids, the sibling group as a whole, and how to map that to a skillful plan so that our co-parenting matches who our children actually are and what they need.

Two other terms you use are: "guest parent" and "duty parent." What do those mean?

I use "guest parent" and "duty parent" to help parents stay out of competition and conflict. We have a residential schedule, and let's just say I am on duty this weekend. The kids are with me. They're in residence with me, but we're at a soccer game. Okay? We're both there, and one of our *kidlets* is on the field, and two of our *kidlets* are in the stands. Of course, I say to the two of them with me in the stands, "Hey, there's your dad. Go say 'hi'." They greet him, cuddle him, and all that good stuff. Then, they say, "Dad, can we go to the snack shack? Will you give us money for ice cream?" Can you picture the scene? Right?

Now, there are couple ways you could respond to that. You could say, "I give your mother child support for that. You go ask your mother. It's her job to be buying that." That would be one response. By the way, not the right one! Here's a different one. You say, "Hey, you know what? Mom's on duty, so you need to go check with mom. I have no idea what her plans are for lunch with you guys, so go over and ask mom. If she says it's okay, if she wants me to take you, I'm happy to."

I am going to respect the residential parent. They're the decision-maker. It minimizes conflict. It's now the end of the game. Makenzie comes off the soccer field. You go over, high-five her. Tell her what a great game she had, and then you say, "Mom is waiting for you," so that there's no disruption to the transition. Again, we're not competing. We are coordinating. I'm on duty. You are the guest. That's how it works.

That's a great way to handle it, Karen, and it brings up another question. Sometimes a child—often at the encouragement of the other parent—may ask the parent for money to pay for something beyond what is covered by child support. The parents haven't discussed this or agreed on anything, but the parent feels pressured and doesn't want to come across like the "mean" parent. How should the parent handle this situation?

That's a really great question. Parents need to get very comfortable saying, "Your mom and I," "Your dad and I," and it goes just like this, "You know what? I hear you. You want to ... yeah. I hear you want to do the ski bus again this year, but you know what? Mom and I have not had a chance to talk about that, so, when we have our meeting, we'll talk about the ski bus, and we'll both get back to you."

Again, we keep executive team information where it belongs. We keep kids where they belong. I'm not going to compete with you by telling them that I think being on the ski bus is great before I know whether you can support that on your time, number one, or if you can afford it, number two. Why would I throw you under the bus? To look like the good parent? How is that good for kids? Right?

Our ability to decide things together and hold back our enthusiasm—I always use that spring break trip, junior year, Washington, DC trip, that whole thing that kids get to do in high school, [as an example]. They come running to the door and say, "Hey, this is going to happen. Can I do it? Can I do it?" You say, "Wow, that's exciting, but you know what? Your mom and I (your dad and I), we'll need to talk about it, and we'll get back to you." There you go. Those extraordinary expenses, no matter what they are, we're going to have those planning meetings. We're going to plan. We're going to talk. We'll decide. We'll follow through. Keep a good credit rating with your co-parent.

That's perfect. A simple response is: "Your mom and I, or your dad and I, have to talk about it."

Which is exactly what we would've said before the divorce. Why are we not saying it now?

Thank you, Karen, for sharing your amazing wisdom and insights. In closing, I have one last question: Communication issues will always arise between co-parents; do you have any final words of advice for parents to help them maintain healthy lines of communication?

Absolutely. I encourage parents to use a business or a colleague-style communication style with one another. I also rely on Bill Eddy's BIFF—brief, informative, friendly and firm—which helps ensure your communication is always polite and, most importantly, child-centered.

There's no reason for you to comment on your co-parent's individual life. You are no longer connected as adults, so let that part go. That being said, if we're child-centered, we're respectful and we've established healthy boundaries, we're going to be brief. Don't go on and on, and on, and on, and on. Brief.

We're going to be informative. "Here's the situation. Here is my question. Here is my thought. Can you help me with that?"

We're going to be firm, so in other words, "Hey, I need to have child care on the weekend, because I'm going to be in a conference. I'm wondering if you're available." I'm going to be clear, direct, firm, but I'm also going to be friendly, so I might close with, "Hey, thanks for considering this. I look forward to hearing back."

The other thing I ask if you are the receiving parent, please respond within 24 hours. If at all possible, you should create a designated co-parent email that you look at once a day—not that you should be getting emails every day, because you shouldn't. However, there are those occasional times where there is something that your co-parent actually needs you to respond to. Diminish the number of texts. We diminish the phone calls because guess what? Your lives, you're trying to separate, but if we have a way to make sure that kids' lives can move forward with clear communication, colleague-style, like you were going to talk to your own boss, we're going to be in really good territory.

To learn more about Karen Bonnell's training, services, books and other resources, visit the Coach Mediate Consult (CMC) website — www.coachmediateconsult.com — and "like" her Facebook page, www.facebook.com/karenbonnellcmc. You may also reach Karen by phone at her office in the greater Seattle area by calling (425) 454-4510.

ABOUT KAREN BONNELL ARNP, MS

Karen Bonnell has over 25 years of experience working with individuals, couples, and families facing transition, loss, stress and change. Karen is the author of the Amazon #1 best -selling book "The Co-Parents' Handbook: Raising Well-Adjusted, Resilient and Resourceful Kids in a Two-Home Family from Little Ones to Young Adults" and "The Parenting Plan Handbook: Four Coaching Seminars devoted to Skillfully Building a Strong, Child-Centered Parenting Plan".

A graduate of the University of Michigan, Karen has been Board certified and licensed as an Advanced Registered Nurse Practitioner since 1982. She served on the faculty of the University of Michigan, Eastern Michigan University & Seattle Pacific University before beginning full-time private practice in 1984. She continues to be a provider of professional continuing education to both healthcare and legal professionals.

Karen played an instrumental role in developing the year-long facilitator training program for the Compassionate Listening Project. As a certified

Compassionate Listening trainer, Karen utilizes this heart-centered approach to authentic speaking and capable listening used around the world in high-conflict situations such as Israel/Palestine.

Karen served on the Board of King County Collaborative Law and Collaborative Professionals of Washington. She is a member of the International Academy of Collaborative Professionals and Academy of Professional Family Mediators.

BUSINESS: Coach | Mediate | Consult

WEBSITE: www.coachmediateconsult.com

EMAIL: karen@coachmediateconsult.com

PHONE: 425.454.4510

LOCATION: Bellevue, WA

FACEBOOK: www.facebook.com/KarenBonnellCMC

TWITTER: www.twitter.com/KarenBonnellCMC

LINKEDIN: www.linkedin.com/in/KarenBonnell

YOUTUBE: www.youtube.com/user/KarenBonnell

PINTEREST: www.pinterest.com/WordsOfArtBlog

CHAPTER FOUR

Using Mediation to Build a Happy Blended Family

by Amanda D. Singer And Jennifer M. Segura

BLENDED FAMILIES

Woven together by Choice, Strengthened by Love, Tested by Everything and Each uniquely Ours

Who doesn't remember the show, "The Brady Bunch"? Corny and kitschy, the show portrayed the near-perfect "blended family". Mike Brady, a widowed architect, and father of three sons, marries Carol Martin, who herself brings three bubbly daughters to the union. Midway through the first season, Carol reassures son, Bobby — who is feeling a bit insecure in his newly evolving role — that she adores him just as she would if he were her biological son:

> **Bobby:** Nobody said goodbye to me or anything, and I didn't think they cared.

Carol: Oh sweetheart, everybody cares. And I bet you your baseball cards, you can't guess who cares the most?

Bobby: You? [Carol nods] Even though I'm only a step?

Carol: Listen, the only steps in this house are those [Carol points to the stairs], the ones that lead up to your bedroom. So how about marching right back up there?

Bobby: Hey Dad, Mom and I are back home again!

Mike: Good, cause that's where you both belong!

In the real world, rare is it that blended family dynamics are as easy as they were on "The Brady Bunch". As anyone who has remarried can attest to, managing blended family dynamics can be complex. It presents unique challenges we're often not prepared for complicated scheduling, issues with exes, stepsibling rivalries are just a few issues you're likely to encounter. While most stepparents and stepchildren develop a genuine mutual affection for each other, at times it can be rocky. Add to the mix, that the rate of divorce for second and third marriages exceeds 60% and 70% respectively.

The elevated divorce rates for remarriages should be cautionary, that if we are a parent in a blended family, we should be cognizant of the challenges we may face and proactively work to create conditions in which the relationship will not only survive, but thrive. Amanda Singer and Jennifer Segura, of the San Diego Family Mediation Center, have developed a successful mediation practice helping all sorts of families and couples in times of transition or crisis. Inspired by experiences in their own personal and professional lives, they've developed an expertise in helping blended families implement sound strategies to effectively communicate and manage conflict.

In the following interview, Amanda and Jennifer share insights from their professional and personal experience working with blended families. Embracing the mantra "Resolve, Rebuild and Renew: Your Family, Your Way", Amanda and Jennifer provide advice on how to:

- Deal with conflict in a constructive way.

- Improve communication, solve problems and reach agreements on legal and non-legal issues.

- Employ compassion and empathy into what is all too often a contentious and adversarial process.

- Stay out of court and remain in control of your future so that you can save time, money, and heartache.

- Get to the heart of the issues that are causing conflict in their relationships.

In the first part of our conversation, Amanda and Jennifer will share their inspiration behind the San Diego Family Mediation Center, the types of families they work with and the services they offer. Then we'll drill down more specifically on issues unique to blended families.

Meet Amanda & Jennifer

Jeremy: Can you share a little bit about what you do at the San Diego Family Mediation Center and the types of clientele you help serve?

Jennifer: We work with families to help them deal with conflict in a constructive way. We try and facilitate ways to improve communication, for them to solve problems, and reach agreements both on legal and non-legal issues. We help families at all different transition times in their lives through premarital mediation, post-marital mediation, and divorce mediation, as well as blended family mediation.

We really work to get at what the heart of the issues is, without going too far into the past and bringing up old wounds. We try to use what we have learned as mediators to help our clients establish new relationships that focus on going forward, and having a mutual respect and understanding of their new roles in each other's lives, whether it's now mother and step-child, or co-parents, instead of husband and wife.

Amanda and I have over 15 years of experience working with families between us. We try to prepare a framework for them to move forward in an amicable manner. We're both law school graduates, we're both Certified Divorce Financial Analysts, we have extensive training in family mediation, and we have worked together for about five years helping families.

What inspired you to get into this field? How did you two get into this field in the first place?

Amanda: I decided I wanted to work in this field when I was in college. I took a class on Dispute Resolution and it was really the first time that I had really heard about the different ideas of mediation or arbitration or negotiation. I liked how it combined law, therapy, and problem-solving, and it was a way to really help people maintain their relationships, instead of tearing them apart.

So when I went to Law School, I did my Master in Dispute Resolution at Pepperdine University. They have a really good Dispute Resolution program there. While I was learning the legal side of things and how to help there, I also took classes in the psychology of conflict and communication and conflict and really learned how to better understand how people communicate and what they're actually saying—their nonverbal versus their verbal cues and what they mean.

On top of that, both Jen and I had other work experience before we went to Law School, working with people. I worked a lot with families and kids. Those experiences continue into your studies and help you better understand what you're being taught and how to implement it.

Also, in Law School, we were able to do some mediation and really get that experience of working directly with people, which a lot of law schools don't do. It's really frustrating that law students come out of school and they have no experience working with clients.

Jennifer: Mine was very similar. It was one of my psychology college classes. We were exploring the Cheyenne Indian Tribe and how their justice system works, and it was a form of mediation. Once I got into that cusp, I realized that was really where I wanted my focus to be. So, I knew going into Law School I wanted to be a mediator and not a litigator, but I also knew that a Legal Education was going to be important for family mediation because there many types of law overlapped with divorce law.

Most attorneys don't come out of school with any hands-on experience?

Amanda: That's right, most law schools don't do what we would call a clinic. When I was in law school we had a lot of different clinics, one of which was a mediation clinic. We had that hands-on experience, but I know most law schools in the country, they just don't. I think some are moving more that way, but there's such an entrenched way of you teaching law where you just have to learn cases and take tests and that's it.

Pre-marital Mediation and Post-marital Mediation

Two of the services you provide are pre-marital mediation and post-marital mediation. Can you expand on what each of these entail?

Jennifer: In pre-marital mediation, clients will come in and we will help them put together their premarital agreement based on what their desires are going forward into the marriage. Some of it may be even financial planning to kind of get an idea of what each of their habits are and what's different between them. Basically, to help bring those issues to the table prior to getting married, so it's not a big surprise that one is a spender and one of them is a saver, for example. Then we help them put together their premarital agreement they can take to their own independent attorneys to review prior to the wedding.

For post-marital, often times we have people come in who, although they were coming in for a divorce, they really aren't ready to necessarily divorce. They just don't know what to do anymore with the problems they have, so we kind of shift gears and say "Well, let's talk about some of these issues and see if we can get you guys to the same page." We may put some of the agreements in writing and prepare what's called a "marital agreement" to keep each partner honest in doing what they say they're going to do; knowing that if they can't adhere to what they've agreed to in mediation, the next step would be a divorce.

Interesting, because when people hear, "premarital mediation", they may think of prenuptial agreements as an agreement to protect one party's assets. I like how you articulated it. It sounds more like you're setting expectations for the relationship. Is that correct?

Amanda: Exactly. The idea with premarital mediation is more just to have a conversation and make sure you're communicating and you know the prenuptial can still be a legally binding document. They have it reviewed and they do what they need to there, but they're doing it together, so there's not this kind of feeling of one person wants it to protect their assets and the other one doesn't.

Blended Family Basics

Through your practice, the two of you serve the needs of any family or couple going through a period of transition or crisis. However, you've also created a bit of a niche by filling a need you've identified, and that is working with "blended families." Before we dive deep into this work, recognizing that terms mean different things to different people, how would you define the term, "blended family"?

Jennifer: That's very true, definitions can vary and we work with a diverse cross-section of families who define it in different ways. Ultimately, it's going to be what it means to them. The common thread we see is a committed adult couple in which one or both of them have a child from a previous relationship.

The adults can be married, they can be cohabitating, they can be opposite sex or same sex. We've worked with all sorts of blended families, and they can vary due to their cultural backgrounds. It's not unusual for there to be step-aunts, step-grandparents who are actively involved. Every family is unique, and it really depends on how they define their family. It's always evolving and we see many different kinds of dynamics.

Millions of Americans are in "blended family" situations, yet I don't think most people are aware that there are mediators such as yourselves who have made working with these families a core part of their practice. What was the catalyst behind your decision to offer services to "blended families"?

Amanda: Our blended family mediation really came about because we saw there was a need. We had a client who called asking for help in combining two families. We found when working with families through divorce, we'd hear they were having issues when there were new partners and they were starting new families. Our clients were finding it difficult to figure out how to take their old families and their new families and work together. There are so many unique challenges that arise when two families combine. We thought using mediation, as we'd done in premarital and divorce situations, was also a great way to help our clients have these conversations so they can build a strong foundation to work on moving forward together. It's really resonated with the families.

What are some of the unique challenges facing blended families and what does a blended family mediation look like?

Amanda: In a blended family there are obviously more people involved in parental roles, and predictably they often have different ideas on what is best for their family. We aim to help them blend all these different ideas into a complementary, cohesive plan that all parties are happy with.

Typically, but not always, we will have four parents involved: two former spouses and two current spouses. Of course, there could be fewer, but this scenario is pretty typical. Jennifer and I work as a team together to identify where the families are encountering the most difficulties and tension so that we can focus our efforts on resolving these issues.

Also, we find it's helpful to identify not just areas where there may be conflict, but where their values, aspirations, and goals intersect, so we can work from a place where there is common ground. We'll ask them questions to reveal areas that they may bond together, for example, we often ask, "what was a significant challenge you encountered in your life and how did you overcome it?" The answer to this question helps them see each other as a person, rather than seeing them simply as this annoying entity that creates issues in their life.

After we work with each group, we take the ex-spouses together and provide them a forum to discuss issues that are on their minds. We identify common goals, where there are issues, where communication needs the most improvement, and what we can do to help.

Jennifer: Like Amanda said, every family situation is unique, although we do come across some common challenges when working with blended families. One of the biggest is when the children don't know where they belong in the family anymore. For instance, when I was sixteen I became part of a blended family. I had originally been the only girl in the family, then my father married someone who had a daughter my exact age and with my name. So now, all of a sudden I wasn't the only girl in the family and I was sharing my dad with another girl my age named Jennifer.

As a child, you start to feel very lost. There's this sense of, "This is where I've always been in my family and now where do I belong?" It's important for the parents and the new parents to really focus on helping the children get through this. I still remember my parents discussing divorcing because of the stress of the kids and trying to get us to all get along because the conflict just gets so bad.

That's one of our biggest issues is the children feeling they're still important in the parent's life, as well as the parent also struggling with the jealousy between their child and their new spouse; trying to get everybody to a place where they want to come together and try and help each other to all get along. Many times, there's just so much tension and anxiety involved that a lot of them don't even want to try.

That's interesting. I can just imagine the uniqueness of these blended families, like the Brady Bunch, right? Two families where each child occupies their own space, maybe you're the oldest kid or you're the youngest kid and then all of a sudden, now you're not.

Jennifer: That's exactly right.

Inevitably, there will be a lot of different issues and helping families navigate these issues requires a unique skill set. You need to blend law, conflict resolution, psychology, compassion and empathy to navigate these waters, right?

Jennifer: Absolutely.

And, law schools typically don't teach this?

Jennifer: No, unfortunately, they don't.

I find it interesting — if not problematic — that most law schools don't teach these skills. I had a conversation with Mark Baer, who wrote an article saying there should be a screen for empathy among attorneys. He said the problem with the legal field is that it draws a significant number of people who are lacking in emotional intelligence, in empathy and compassion.

What I think truly separates you and Amanda apart is you knew you wanted to do this from the very, very beginning. You were on the path of conciliatory mediation, ways to find bridges.

Jennifer: That's our goal, to build bridges. And in this field, working with families that may be experiencing a crisis, or crises, to effectively help families, you need a strong sense of compassion and empathy.

Blended Family Mediation

Unfortunately, it does seem there is a lack of societal awareness around mediation. Too often, we reflexively think we have to litigate everything; that we have to go through the courts for every single thing when, in fact, that's not the case at all. If you have two willing, cooperative parents, they can extricate themselves from the adversarial family court process at any time they want, use services like yours and save themselves so much time, money and heartache.

Jennifer: Right, and the more people do mediation, have success with it, the more they will tell their friends about it. Then we'll see more people using this process. The court is not a place for families to be. It's not suited for children and parents trying to figure out what to do with their everyday lives.

No, it's not. It's a place for litigants, not families. Family court is not a place where a lot of healing occurs.

Now let me ask, while mediation is clearly a far less adversarial process than family court, but there are still challenges. What are some of the challenges you face, or that families deal with when they're going to mediation?

Amanda: Sometimes it can definitely be hard to get everyone to agree. We know that everyone in the family loves the children and we want to help them reframe the issues to focus on the kids because the children may feel as though they're not sure where they belong. For the kids, seeing their parents have these important conversations, it really lets them know their needs are valued. We find no one's going to disagree about wanting what's best for their kid, so if you can always keep the kids front and center, it really helps us.

I think the most important thing that we do with our clients — knowing that every situation is different, every family is different — is we work our models to find what is going to work with them. Really the biggest thing is putting the children front and center. Realizing they can find ways to work together to benefit the children also benefits the parents.

We also want to help the parents stop rehashing the past. A lot of times, people come in and they just want to keep talking about everything the other person did wrong and what they're not good at. Instead, we want to focus on reinforcing the positive co-parenting skills. We want to highlight the good qualities they have and help them really address the root of the conflict.

> *"We also want to help the parents stop rehashing the past. A lot of times, people come in and they just want to keep talking about everything the other person did wrong and what they're not good at."*

Jennifer: We had two women come in who'd had a child together while they were married. Now they were divorced and each of them had new partners in their lives. All four of them came in to discuss the parenting plan between the two initial parents and how their new spouses would be involved in raising their child. We were able to help them nail down some of the main issues, as well as come up with some solutions moving forward.

A lot of their issues stemmed from a lack of communication and misunderstanding about things that had been said and done. Giving them a room to sit in to have these conversations where all four of them could actually participate — so the new spouse is not at home hearing secondhand what happened — was very helpful and provided them with tools to use in the future if the communication starts to break down again. Giving them tools to use to clear the air and better communicate going forward really seemed to help them.

Are there any circumstances where mediation is not appropriate, or it may be appropriate, but requires additional considerations?

Jennifer: In a situation where one of the parents was a violent abuser and the other parent fears for their safety, this dynamic generally wouldn't lend itself well to mediation.

Also, in situations where there is a significant power imbalance where one parent is always going to give into the other parent's demands and not be aware of their rights, this sort of situation is far more challenging in mediation. However, even in this type of situation, mediation can still be of tremendous benefit, but to alleviate that power balance, each parent may need to be represented by their own attorneys so that one of the parents does not fall victim to the power imbalance.

The challenge is that if there is a power imbalance, there's not one person advocating for the parent that has the lesser power. Whereas, if they have an attorney, they have someone advocating on their behalf who can protect their interest—basically, it's a hybrid between mediation and the attorney represented model.

Parents should keep in mind that in mediation, we don't represent either parent, but rather, we're a neutral third party. We're not going to tell either parent definitively, "This is in your best interest." But even in a mediation without attorneys, we encourage parents to make the decision they want; they can do things that are different from what their legal right may be, but we want them to be aware of all the potential outcomes so that they can make an informed, educated decision.

Achieving Harmony in a Blended Family

What advice do you recommend to parents in blended family situations?

Jennifer: Children need to feel comfortable expressing their feelings and emotions. Give them permission to be upset. Allow them to express anger or frustration in a healthy, constructive manner. And, if they need additional support, such as therapy, be open to providing them the support they need, whatever support they need to get through things and be emotionally healthy.

> *"Allow them to express anger or frustration in a healthy, constructive manner."*

Also, recognize it takes time. It can often take two or more years; sometimes it can take up to 8 years for that blended family life cycle to get to a phase where they all feel like a family and have that loyalty to each other. In those first couple of years, there's going to be more turmoil. That's okay. Family members are adapting to a new structure and new rules, so time is probably the greatest factor to consider.

Know that nothing happens overnight, but it will get better, and by employing patience, sensitivity, and empathy, parents can accelerate the time it takes. But, give children space they need to go at their own pace. You don't need to rush them or express dissatisfaction that they're not adapting quickly enough. Two to eight years is a pretty common period of transition, assimilation, and adjustment.

In psychology, when looking at grief or loss, psychologists identify various stages of recovery. I'm curious, are there different identifiable stages that blended families go through as they strengthen their family unit?

Jennifer: Definitely. Typically, we see three phases that blended families go through:

Immersion Phase: During the immersion phase, everything is very new. Sometimes it can be a very happy phase. Other times it can be a challenge as everyone adapts to what is a brand new situation. There could be feelings of uneasiness or that something is wrong; it's not uncommon for a parent or a child to fault themselves for any conflict or uneasiness that may be present.

Mobilization or Action Phase: During this phase, relationships begin to mature and bonds strengthen. However, it's not always smooth sailing. As parents and children feel more open expressing themselves, it can be a chaotic or embattled period. During this phase, family dynamics can evolve as boundaries are established.

Generally, enough understanding has evolved in the family that activities are no longer power struggles between the outsiders and insiders. But, it can also be a period that is stressful.

Resolution Phase: During the resolution phase, there's a sense of unity and cohesion in the family unit. The family feels solid and the relationships between family members are predictable and reliable. While some children may feel more inside or less inside the family, generally there is a sense of acceptance of this reality.

It's important to note that each phase can take different amounts of time; progression through each stage does not occur magically or necessarily neatly. Also, factors like whether or not the kids are dealing with other issues—perhaps difficulty at school, conflict between siblings or parents, substance abuse. Any of those issues can create more turmoil that will take more time to resolve, and therapy can be beneficial to help families who get stuck or don't feel as if they're progressing as they'd like to.

What are some common myths you encounter?

Jennifer: One of the biggest myths is that there isn't much difference between blended families and biological families. In fact, life is quite different. In a blended family, you don't have that previous history together. When working with these families, in some ways, it's like a merger of two companies. You have to figure out how they're going to work together and the goal is to make it a friendly merger.

Another big myth is that loving and caring will happen instantly. People ask, "why hasn't this happened right away?" But, it takes time. If the children are younger, it can be easier because they have fewer memories and may adapt easier. When the kids are older, it can be harder for the kids to want to accept the change because once you're older, you've known things the way they once were so you may not be to understand why they're happening the way they are now happening.

Overcoming Challenges

Do you ever have to deal with situations in which one of the parents has lingering jealousy towards the other parent's new partner, even though they're both re-partnered?

Jennifer: In one situation, I had a set of couples in which it seemed like that was going on. Although, I think the ex-wife wasn't really jealous in the sense that she wanted her ex-husband back. I think the jealousy was over the fact that he and his new partner were making it work and the two of them hadn't been able to. I think just seeing your ex-spouse be in a positive relationship that's working can make the other spouse jealous, wondering, "Well, why wasn't I good enough?" or "Why couldn't we make this work?"

That's an excellent point. If you were in a relationship with someone and that relationship failed, and that person is now in a relationship that's successful and thriving, there could be a natural instinct to

go, "What the heck? Why is he or she able to make it, why are they thriving?" Or, you can be happy for your ex, because "Hey, we just didn't have the chemistry." It's a choice and you can interpret the situation either way, but if you choose to dwell on the negative, you will feel like a failure.

Amanda: Exactly, people make a choice how they decide to interpret events, and they can focus on the positive, or focus on the negative. But, ultimately, if we stay focused on our children's needs, rather than our own unresolved feelings, everyone will be better off.

In that same situation, their daughter, the joint daughter between the two families, had begun calling the new step-mom, "mom". They hadn't encouraged it, it just kind of happened. The other mom, the biological mom, was hurt by that and wanted them to not encourage that to happen, but at the same time, how do you tell a nine-year-old not to? You have to give them the ability to do what feels natural to them.

Family court isn't equipped — nor was it designed — to help families manage conflict. It's court. It's adversarial. You have two parties suing each other. That being said, I believe most judges would prefer that families work out their issues and resolve conflict outside of court, and the role of the judge should essentially entail signing off on agreements made outside of courts.

Most judges recognize they are legal professionals, not family therapists, and other professionals are better equipped to work with families outside the court. However, outside the basic minimal family court mediation that is mandated in most family courts, most families don't take advantage of private mediation.

How do we get more families to follow the mediation path rather than rely on the family court system?

Amanda: I think the best way is to educate parents, generate awareness that mediation is an option and an alternative that provides better outcomes than litigating through family court.

> *"...mediation is an option and an alternative that provides better outcomes than litigating through family court."*

Sometimes parents have an irrational fear about the process, about of having to sit across from who they may perceive as their adversary, but usually, this fear is overblown. This person is not your adversary, they usually share the same goals as you. And, when parents consider how much better an experience mediation is compared to court — court is almost always far more expensive, emotionally draining and potentially destructive — choosing mediation becomes an easy choice.

When we meet with clients who are unsure whether or not they should use mediation, we ask, "How is what you're doing now working for you?" And, the answer is almost always, "It's not." We then help them understand how they can resolve their issues through mediation, and, of course, the fact that they can save themselves a lot of time, money and pain by avoiding court.

Amanda. Jennifer. Thank you so much for sharing your insights!

Amanda Singer and Jennifer Segura work with families during all phases of the relationship life cycle, from pre-marriage through post-marriage reconciliation and mediation. If you want to learn more or schedule a free consultation with the San Diego Family Mediation Center, you may reach Amanda or Jennifer at (858) 736-2411 or visit their website www. SanDiegoFamilyMediationCenter.com. They're always happy to answer any questions and make sure families are able to get the information they need.

ABOUT AMANDA D. SINGER, Esq., MDR, CDFA™ & JENNIFER M. SEGURA, JD, CDFA™

AMANDA D. SINGER, Esq., MDR, CDFA™

Amanda Singer has long been passionate about assisting families in working through their conflict together and staying out of court. She has been a part of San Diego Family Mediation Center for over three years helping families improve communications, solve problems and reach agreements.

Prior to her current role with San Diego Family Mediation Center, Amanda was a divorce mediator for The Divorce Help Clinic and worked at the San Diego North County Family Law Facilitator's Office helping self-represented litigants with their family law issues.

Amanda earned her bachelor's in Sociology from Brandeis University. After graduation, she moved to California to earn her JD from Chapman University School of Law while completing her Masters in Dispute

Resolution (MDR) from The Straus Institute of Dispute Resolution at Pepperdine University School of Law. She is also a Certified Divorce Financial Analyst (CDFA).

Amanda is a member of the State Bar of California, the American Bar Association, San Diego County Bar Association, San Diego Family Law Bar Association, Lawyers Club of San Diego and The Academy of Professional Family Mediation.

JENNIFER M. SEGURA, JD, CDFA™

Jennifer Segura has dedicated her professional life to mediation and helping families resolve conflict. Trained as a family mediator, she opened San Diego Family Mediation Center in January 2007 and has solely practiced as a family mediator since that time.

In October 2009, Jennifer was hired by The Divorce Help Clinic as the head mediator. In 2015, she decided to focus full-time on growing San Diego Family Mediation. After realizing some of the most complex issues involved in a divorce are financial, Jennifer became a Certified Divorce Financial Analyst (CDFA) in 2012. This certification has given Jennifer the ability to help clients explore creative ideas while knowing the tax and other financial ramifications that may apply under each scenario.

Jennifer began her undergraduate studies at San Diego State University in 1997. She fell in love with San Diego and has been a resident ever since college.

Jennifer attended Thomas Jefferson School of Law and graduated Cum Laude with her Juris Doctor in 2004.

She is a member of the Institute for Divorce Financial Analysts, Association of Divorce Financial Planners and The Academy of Professional Family Mediators.

BUSINESS: San Diego Family Mediation Center

WEBSITE: www.sdfmc.com

EMAIL: info@sandiegofamilymediation.com

PHONE: 858-736-2411

LOCATION: Del Mar, CA

FACEBOOK: www.facebook.com/SanDiegoFamilyMediationCenter

TWITTER: www.twitter.com/SDFMC

CHAPTER FIVE

Approaching Divorce With Mindfulness And Compassion

by Belinda N. Zylberman

> *"If our children are our future, let their 'highest good' guide us in our actions and our thoughts."* —
> *Belinda Zylberman*

Belinda and I first connected in 2014 and we quickly hit it off—we embrace similar values and a shared passion for bringing awareness to parents going through a divorce, that there's a healthier and more mindful way to approach the process than suing each other in family court. Immediately, I sensed Belinda's altruism and passion for helping families in transition and crisis—a passion spawned from her own personal life experiences. Belinda blends compassion, empathy and professionalism to create as harmonious an experience as one could hope for going through a process that too often lends itself to pain and anguish.

Part of what makes Belinda unique is that she believes divorce need not be this incredibly painful experience, that by approaching our circumstances with intention, empathy, and an open mind, we can treat divorce as one of life's transitional events that offers an opportunity for transformative growth.

Moreover, if we employ mindfulness, maintain self-awareness and recognize that our behaviors and actions impact our children, we can achieve outcomes that will promote the emotional health of all those involved, particularly our children. As Belinda shared with me, "When you're getting divorced and you're ending the relationship as husband and wife, you're moving into a new relationship, as co-parents. A relationship continues to exist, let's not be mistaken otherwise - it's just evolving and becoming something different."

Through our conversation, Belinda shares the knowledge she's acquired over years of study and working with families, including:

- How to approach divorce with compassion and be intentional about the process so that you can achieve the best outcome for yourself and your children.

- How to employ the mindfulness that's integral to being a parent, recognizing that even our most subtle actions and behaviors impact our children.

- How to view divorce as a potentially positive transitional period that provides an opportunity for developing greater self-awareness, growth, and healing.

Employing the knowledge and skills she obtained from law school, her master's work in spiritual psychology and several hundred hours of mediation training, Belinda has helped hundreds of families achieve desirable outcomes that serve our common aspirations of creating nurturing and emotionally healthy family dynamics.

Meet Belinda

Jeremy: Hi, Belinda. In previous conversations we've had, you shared with me your passion around this work, and how several life experiences, both as a child and as an adult, inspired you to get into this field and help families in transition work through issues in a mindful manner. How did you get started in mediation and what specifically inspired you to do the work that you do?

Belinda: I did my undergraduate studies in Communications and Anthropology and then I attended law school. I think back then I had sort of this "save the world" mentality and was passionate about people and our relationships to one another. Then I entered a relationship, got married, and then divorced. When I was re-partnering, I met a man who was going through a divorce himself, but with two kids. The difference in our situations was that he had kids, and I didn't. The fact that there were kids involved—and I really loved these kids—made me think a little differently about how divorce impacts kids and the impact of divorce itself.

As I was going through this process with this man and his children (and their mom), we were searching for resources and people with whom to create a support structure within which to go through this experience. What we found was pretty negative. People were basically telling us, "Your kids are doomed." They had all kinds of things to say about the step-mom role and just a lot of negative things to say about divorce in general. We kind of looked at each other and said, "This doesn't feel right. Too many people are in the same situation as us and we can't all be doomed."

That same year I was certified in divorce mediation. That was fourteen years ago and I have been passionately doing this work ever since.

Tell me a little bit about Paikea Mediation, the types of people you help, and what kinds of outcomes you seek to help them achieve.

Paikea Mediation is a family and divorce mediation practice. The majority of my work centers around families going through divorce. I prefer working with couples that have kids because I have observed over time the parents' desire to be as intentional as possible about the process. There is a mindfulness that goes with being a parent and recognizing your actions and behaviors impact your children, and that they are looking to you as their role models.

The outcome I aim to serve with the families I work with are well written, well thought out agreements that serve not just the best interest of the kids, but also the best interest of the parents. I think we'll be talking a lot about that, but it's really important in the divorcing process that we don't forget Mom and Dad. Divorcing spouses deserve to have positive outcomes out of this challenging experience as well.

Overcome Obstacles, Be Intentional and Minimize Conflict

What is the most common obstacle that prevents parents from achieving an outcome they'll be happy with—not just at the end of the divorce, but in the long term?

I think the most common obstacle is one that's not obvious to most people at the start of the divorce process. People enter the process in a variety of ways: with a lawyer, with a mediator, or maybe they're trying to sit down and figure it out themselves. But what they all have in common is their stories—the stories of people they know who went through a divorce, the stories they've heard on the news or read online. And more often than not, these stories instigate fear and "against-ness." This can lead to a lot of unproductive conversations for a couple that is committed to making conscious decisions around their divorce.

This can then often become the biggest obstacle in terms of the mindset with which people enter their divorce. I can't tell you how many times people come in wanting to give mediation a try because they have this sense the divorce could happen in a mindful, even loving or caring way, or, at least, an intentional way. But in the back of their mind, they're positioning. They're thinking "let me make sure I've got the best lawyer in town so my spouse can't get that person first," or "if she's not reasonable about this situation, I'm getting a lawyer. I'll just take her to court and we'll duke it out."

I think that kind of fire is very much fueled by the environment and the discussion that is still prevalent in our society around divorce. Divorce continues to be viewed as a win/lose kind of situation to be in as opposed to neutralizing it a bit, and looking at it more simply and perhaps more honestly as a transition that some of us go through in our lives—a big change that some of us go through—but one that can be done with dignity, care, and intention, and that can actually produce long-term, positive results, both for the individuals that are separating as well as the kids and the other people who are impacted.

Those are great points, and I like what you said in terms of, if not loving, at least, be intentional because so often parents get caught up in the moment, and the anger and the resentments manifest or surface during the divorce process. As you said, they could be thinking in their mind, positioning for having the best attorney. It's really this sort of adversarial win/lose process rather than the more healing, therapeutic process you're promoting.

Are there any specific examples from your professional experience where you've worked with a family getting too caught up in the conflict, yet you were able to help them ultimately achieve an outcome that was best for them and, most importantly, for their children?

Your question reminds me of the first case I had when I first opened my practice in Portland. I was working with a family with two small children. They had gone the way of hiring attorneys because they didn't know any better. I would come to learn, in our first mediation session, that they had spent over $20,000 in the initial filing of papers and the discovery process and they were still nowhere. They were about to enter a round of psychological evaluations where their kids would have to be involved and interviewed, and both parents were dreading this.

It was around the same time the mom heard about me and the work I do and they decided to try mediation. They came in scared about the toll the divorce was going to take on everyone, particularly the children. They were three and five at the time.

This was such a great case for me to learn from because it really highlighted the importance of education and getting people access to resources, of really spreading the word that there are other ways to do this. This was a family that was clearly in conflict, as many families are when entering the divorcing process, but their choice to go down the adversarial path was less a factor of the conflict they were experiencing then a factor of not knowing what other options were out there.

I think for those who are thinking about getting a divorce, have gone through a divorce, or are in the process of getting a divorce, getting educated and choosing the way you want the process to go is extremely important. There are books, professionals, and resources that are part of a growing community focused on supporting people through divorce, who recognize that there's a different way to live this experience—a better way.

Divorce Can Provide an Opportunity for Growth and Healing

Right, and that's a great point you made that a lot of parents just aren't aware because socially we just think, "Okay we have to go down this route that's litigious, or at the very least, we're hiring attorneys," when there is another path that's going to be more beneficial to them and more beneficial to their kids.

You also mentioned you really love this work because during periods of transition there's actually an opportunity for greater awareness, learning, and healing. I think most people would associate divorce with pain, so how is it that you see these transitional periods as opportunities for growth and healing?

It takes me back to when I was a teenager and the experience of my parents' separation, and then some years later, the experience of the deaths of both of my parents. Death and divorce are huge periods of transition, and I have often thought about the meaning of such events. With my parents' separation, I always felt like they didn't really want to talk about it. I was already a teenager and in their minds, it didn't really impact me as I would be heading to college. But I felt like I needed to understand the meaning of it. I needed to understand why things happen. I needed to get underneath it.

When I was going through my own divorce and getting remarried, that came up again for me. That need to understand what I could learn from these transitions and from these experiences was as significant as going through them. I think, for me, living these experiences and then moving into a career where I spend time with people going through transitions - divorce, death, painful and challenging situations - has led me to create a philosophy around the purpose of relationships and the awareness that they exist for our learning, our growth, and our healing as human beings.

In terms of the growth and the healing possibilities that divorce presents, I have observed that with many couples, when we look at the relationship itself as an opportunity for healing and growth, what we discover is that it's the moments of adversity, as much as the moments of joy and connection, that teach us some of our greatest lessons.

> *"...I have observed that with many couples, when we look at the relationship itself as an opportunity for healing and growth, what we discover is that it's the moments of adversity, as much as the moments of joy and connection, that teach us some of our greatest lessons."*

I think the divorce process, can be an incredible time for growth, just as with the passing of a loved one. Many people compare divorce and death, reporting that the feelings can be the same or similar. I think divorce gives us this moment in time to stop, reevaluate, and consider our lives—through the pain. And we're not talking about not feeling the pain, because it is painful and we're having to let go - to let go of long-held hopes and dreams, to let go of a way we viewed our life. And then to be thrust into having to think about life as a single parent, as divorced men and women, and as alone. To have to think about our lives in a way we never wanted to have to consider.

I think this is where reflection and time redeem us. Learning to view the situation from the perspective that the relationship is not over, but rather transitioning, all of our relationships come become about healing, and growth, and learning. When we are getting divorced, one of the things I always share with parents in the first session is, "You're getting divorced and you're ending your married relationship, but you're moving into a relationship as co-parents. There is still a relationship there. Let's not be mistaken. There continues to be a relationship, it's simply evolving and becoming something else. So why not then consider the possibility that this relationship is an opportunity for healing and growth, as it will be a relationship that's going to be with you for many years to come."

> *"So why not then consider the possibility that this relationship is an opportunity for healing and growth, as it will be a relationship that's going to be with you for many years to come."*

That's a great point. It's a theme we try to carry through, that there is a relationship that exists irrespective of what's happening. Whether you're divorced or not, you still have that relationship because you are bound together with your children.

That's right.

Now, you speak a lot about mindful divorce, or a well-lived divorce. Can you expand more on what you mean by a well-lived divorce?

Sure. I think it goes to the point that we were just making. I had new clients in yesterday and as they sat before me I could see that at one point they were on the verge of getting upset and triggered. Soon after, through some discussion and sharing of their feelings, they calmed down and relaxed with each other. In any transition, and divorce is a great example, it is a time of great triggering moments and an opportunity to really experience human emotion.

When I think of a well-lived divorce, I think about a scenario I ask parents early on in the process. I have them imagine their children as young adults, in their 20's, and they are having a conversation with them. I then ask them how they would want this conversation with to go? What would you say to them about your divorce process? About their other parent? I offer all kinds of questions for their consideration because this is their process and questions will elicit different responses depending on the listener. For me, the key is not so much the message they choose to share with their "future children" but the intention with which they experience the future experience in the scenario. This exercise can serve to shift the parents' entire view of the divorce, which is happening in the present. As they turn to each other after going through this process (as they often do), they are heart-centered, humbled and have a mindset to make agreements with everyone's best intentions in mind.

People often don't experience having a "choice" in divorce because one person may be insisting on the divorce while the other may want to work things out. But beyond the initial decision to divorce, I believe we have many choices: choice in how we behave, choice in how we choose to react or not react, choice with our words, and choice in how we are being with ourselves as we go through the process. I think a well-lived divorce is one where we say to ourselves, "I'm giving myself a lot of compassionate self-forgiveness through the process. I'm doing my best to understand what I can. I'm doing the best that I can. I'm looking to my future ex and also saying he/she is doing the best they can. I'm committing to going through this process with awareness."

Now, you mentioned you went through your own divorce and you have children. What are some of the greatest misconceptions you think parents have about the divorce process and how can these misconceptions have a negative impact on children if the parents are not conscious of the potential pitfalls?

Yes. As I mentioned earlier, when I was re-partnering and choosing to be with a man who had children, the literature, our friends and even a well-renowned therapist we saw, all steered us in the direction of doom and gloom. Entering the world of divorce, ex-spouses and step-parenting could only lead down a dark and lonely path. I'll never forget what the therapist said in one of our early sessions, "I have clients in their thirties and they're still angry or upset about their parent's divorce."

I can still feel the pit in my stomach after hearing that and thinking, "Can it really be that this is what we are subjecting them to? Can this truly be the only outcome that's possible? How can we do this to these kids?" I remember we had so much guilt and shame going through that process.

For many people that I see who are ending a marriage and beginning a new relationship, oftentimes it happens that there's not a lot of time between the ending of one and the beginning of another. And questions of uncertainty, guilt and shame with regard to our children can arise so easily. I think the key is turning towards sources, people and a philosophy that support the view that this is a transition and we have a choice about the meaning and interpretations we place on it. Meaning, it is not intrinsically "good" or "bad." The experience is what each of us makes of it.

This makes me think about the example of nature. We have winter, spring, summer, fall. We don't get angry when the trees lose their leaves, or when the snow covers the ground, or when the sun melts the snow. We simply call this nature, which is made up of transitions, and they are natural and neutral.

> *"We have winter, spring, summer, fall. We don't get angry when the trees lose their leaves, or when the snow covers the ground, or when the sun melts the snow. We simply call this nature, which is made up of transitions, and they are natural and neutral."*

Now we could certainly debate all day, and anyone going through a divorce today would have very good reason to say, "How could you possibly say divorce is neutral!" And any reasonable person could argue that it's not — far from it. But perhaps the value to be found here as we engage in another way of viewing divorce, is not in arguing how divorce is an awful, painful terrible thing, but rather, to consider the possibility that it could be something else through mindfulness and intention.

Coaching and Mediation Versus Litigation

Now, you mentioned a lack of awareness that a lot of parents have in terms of methods and what to do when they're getting a divorce. Most parents think the first step when getting a divorce is to hire an attorney as soon as they make that decision.

Two-part question: First, why is it beneficial to hire a professional such as yourself early on in the process? Second, if advising a parent on how to divorce in a manner that will be the least destructive on their children, what process do you recommend?

There are a plethora of professionals and resources out there today that will serve families who want to have a good working co-parenting relationship after the divorce. I think contrary to what a lot of mediators might say, I think going to an attorney early on in the process can be informative to educate you about the law and provide important information about the process - if they are approached for this specific purpose. The key here is how you approach the entire process where lawyers, mediators, and other professionals are there to support you. Specifically, finding a support system and set of professionals that reflect your beliefs about how you want to live your divorce and create the foundation for your future co-parenting relationship.

I think the difference between working with an attorney and working with a mediator is pretty simple. With an attorney, more often than not, you're not face-to-face with your soon-to-be ex. For many people, that's very appealing. You get to have an advocate defending your rights and your position, and you have this barrier or "safety zone" between you and your soon-to-be ex. Of course, what this also means is that you're not having some of the most important conversations of your life with the person you need to be having them with.

> *"I think the difference between working with an attorney and working with a mediator is pretty simple…[it] means that [by working with an attorney] you're not having some of the most important conversations of your life with the person you need to be having them with."*

The mediation process, in its simplest definition, is one where two people, in divorce cases the spouses, are able to come and sit at the table together and have these often life-changing conversations. My intention is to support people in moving towards healing, compassion, understanding and clear agreements. And in my experience, as I observe families moving through the mediation process, they create hope for the future as they work to serve the highest good for everyone involved. Mediation can and does create that opportunity for families.

What I want to make really clear is that whether it's an attorney or mediator, or another professional you choose to support you in this process, getting yourself educated is the key. Doing enough research and really asking the important questions including, "How do I want to go through this process? What kind of support do I think I need? Who would be the person best to support me?"

As I was speaking with the mom in one of the families I mentioned earlier, one of the first things she tells me is that her initial reaction based on information she's getting from friends and family members is to go get the toughest attorney who can litigate and get everything she wants. I thought, "Wow, okay. I hear her starting point."

That gave me a lot of information about how to go forward with this couple. Attorneys works the way they work, we've all heard horror stories and good ones alike, and that route will work for some people. But in my experience, for the majority of people today who are being more mindful and conscious as they divorce, getting the toughest attorney to litigate is not going to be the route that gets you to solid agreements that support everyone in your family.

You make some great points. First off, what you think you want at the time versus reflecting back maybe five years, ten years from now, that's going to change. It's going to evolve, but may also change in terms of dynamics. It may seem appealing to have this proxy arguing on your behalf; you have basically dissolved that ability to communicate. One of the benefits of mediation is it does preserve that ability to communicate and also for both parents to be heard.

That's right.

Closing Thoughts & Key Takeaways

Belinda, if there was one thing you'd want all parents to know or understand, what would that be?

I think the most important thing is that no matter what anyone's situation is—and I've seen a vast range of family dynamics going through divorce—the thing to remember is that each of us has a lot more ability to affect change in our situation than we might believe we do. When I say this, what I mean is that many times I've sat across from two people and observed that what was most needed was simply the ability to be quiet and listen, or to be open to looking at something in a different way. The person we show up as, and the mindset we choose to have when we're in the situation has everything to do with the resolution of it. And that's very much in our control.

And, what is one lesson you'd want all parents to understand going through this process?

It's a lesson for each of us as parents, and an important one to teach our children: that the event itself (the divorce) is not the issue—it's how we relate to the event as we experience it. When we're talking about a couple entering the divorcing process, and I see time and time again people who come in with clear intention, integrity, and a true willingness and commitment to go through the process. These are the families that create the results they committed to from the beginning. Those couples who come in and are more committed to the past and the hurt, focusing on the blaming and the shaming and the denigration of the relationship, will have to work a lot harder to get those kinds of results.

> *"Those couples who come in and are more committed to the past and the hurt, focusing on the blaming and the shaming and the denigration of the relationship, will have to work a lot harder..."*

What I've learned over time, from personal experience and working with amazing clients, is that when you claim from the beginning that the divorce itself is not what is determining or creating our reactions but rather, our approach to the divorce is, then we are empowered to live the experience as we choose. And one way may be to embrace this as a transition - an event we can fold into the story of our lives, one of many that has shaped us, and one that helps us to know ourselves better.

I think you captured that brilliantly. It's not the event itself but how we choose to go through the event, how we process it, and going through with intention. It's definitely great advice.

Now, finally, you've got another book coming out, and in terms of a lot of people want to reach out to you, how can the reader find out more about how to contact you? Maybe speak a little bit about your book project as well.

Sure. I'm located in Portland, Oregon, and I see mostly local clients. Anyone can reach out to me through my website or contact me via phone. I'm always happy to do a fifteen-minute to thirty-minute free consultation. It's not as easy for me to do face to face mediation with people who have contacted me from around the country (there is skype if people are open to that), but I'm always really happy to hear from anyone and help them with resources and referrals.

In terms of the book, it's pretty exciting. It's tentatively called The New Family Revolution and my intention is for it to be out in the world by the end of 2016. It revolves around this idea of shifting the notion of what it means to be in a family and to be in a relationship. It addresses the landscape of partnership, marriage, and parenting, specifically looking at the unique dynamics people face today as so many of us—perhaps now the majority of the US population—have been touched by divorce.

Belinda lives in Portland, Oregon with her blended family, where in addition to her work as a mediator, she is an author and enjoys yoga, hiking, reading and travel. To learn more about Belinda, read her blog, keep abreast of her latest projects, or hire her, visit her website at www.paikeamediation.com.

ABOUT BELINDA N. ZYLBERMAN, JD

Belinda Zylberman is a compassionate and seasoned divorce mediator whose work revolves around helping clients create "well-lived transitions" with a particular focus on what happens after a divorce, separation, and loss.

Belinda received her undergraduate degree in Communications and Anthropology from the University of Massachusetts and her law degree from Cardozo Law School. Currently, she's completing her second year of a Master's Degree in Spiritual Psychology at the University of Santa Monica.

Additionally, Belinda has over 500 hours of experiential education training, having studied with thought leaders around the world. Belinda spent 10 years of her career working, volunteering and studying abroad, in countries including Bosnia and Herzegovina, Belgium and France and has spent time in 45 countries to date. She attributes much of the success in her work with families and individuals in transition to her experience and exposure to so many languages – spoken and unspoken – and diverse cultures.

BUSINESS: Paikea Mediation

WEBSITE: www.paikeamediation.com

EMAIL: belinda@paikeamediation.com

PHONE: 971.998.6895

LOCATION: Portland, OR

LINKEDIN: www.linkedin.com/in/belindazylberman

The Road to Resiliency: How to Raise Resilient Children Through a Family Transition

by Kristine Clay

"Healing happens in the present." —Kristine Clay

Kristine brings her unique background to help families cope with challenges such as divorce and other life transitions. Having been long interested in how crisis and stress affect the brain, she has studied neuroscience to learn how the brain forms connections, can change by experiences, and how divorce relationship dynamics can impact the "hard wiring" in our children's brains. A significant benefit to Kristine's work is the opportunity to learn how we can potentially "re-wire" our brains with new, positive experiences.

Based on years of research studying attachment, resiliency, conflict, and integrative parenting, Kristine shares her insights to help parents and children cope with stress and achieve balance. She works with divorcing parents to develop strategies to enhance their parent-child relationship and build resiliency and confidence in their children.

In this chapter, you will learn key concepts, including:

- What "resiliency" is and why it's important

- What "attachment" is in children and how it is affected by divorce

- How ongoing conflict can impact children and their attachment relationships

- How divorce or separation can threaten a child's sense of security and what parents can do to create a sense of safety

- What it means to allow "necessary uncomfortableness" and how it can lead to increased resiliency

- How to help your child or children develop resiliency

- Why it is important to allow your child to "tell their own story"

Kristine is based in the greater Puget Sound area of Washington where she is a therapist, parenting coach, and developer of Integrative Parent Coaching, LLC.

Jeremy: "Resiliency" has become a buzzword. How do you define "resiliency" and why is it important?

Kristine: Resiliency is our ability to withstand stress; to recover or bounce back from change, transition, or trauma. Families who go through divorce or conflict endure many losses, stressors, traumas, and multiple changes—both large and small—to their daily life. While both adults and children experience these changes, because children are still developing cognitively, socially and emotionally, they are at an elevated risk to develop a variety of issues. Therefore, as parents, it is important that we are aware of our children's vulnerabilities and needs, and provide them the support and guidance they need to adapt to change and "bounce."

In my work, I am interested in how a child can build these skills with the help of their parent. It's important for parents to act as the principal agents of healing. How we form and sustain these connections, and what we can specifically do to support our children at every developmental stage, varies depending on their age. For example, it looks quite a bit different at age four than it does at age thirteen. Information and research on attachment provide a valuable lens into how the brain develops throughout childhood, and how a parent can alter their actions and reactions with their child to help rewire the brain through experiences that can promote healing.

Parents are often anxious and understandably worried about how their child is doing through a season of divorce. Children pick up on parents' anxieties and may "catch" their worry and anxiety. This is a function of two brains mirroring, communicating on a very deep and implicit level. Helping parents attune to their child and manage their stress can strengthen their relationship and help their child adapt and cope.

"Attachment" and the Needs of Children

What do you mean by attachment and how is it affected by divorce?

Children ask: "Is this my fault? What will happen to me? Am I safe? Will my parent leave me? Does what I want matter?" They have many questions when faced with a change in their family, whether they are experiencing a separation, divorce or custody change.

Regardless of the age of the child, their basic need when faced with adversity is safety and the security and preservation of their attachment relationships. Attachment is the relationship with a parent that provides safety, protection, and comfort. It is essential for survival. Children have attachments from an early age that need to be considered, with both parents and other adults or siblings.

Every child comes into the world helpless and requiring care; they can do nothing for themselves. The infant senses and "feels" this vulnerability and, therefore, cry when they have a need, or coo and look adorable to gain attention. In fact, in cases where a child does not perform these behaviors, it suggests the child has learned that there is no one willing or available to meet their needs, and they have, in a sense, given up. This dance between the baby and caregiver informs them implicitly of the way the world regards them, their sense of self-value, and they learn how much to trust the world and others. They learn if they are protected as well. From that safe place, a child can explore and be curious.

Children develop strategies to secure their attachment figures' regard. Attachment and strategizing to get their security and comfort does not end in infancy. Children rely on their parents as a rock from which to explore and expand their curiosity, even into their teen years.

In unsettling circumstances such as divorce, some children become a caretaker of the parent who is suffering. Others may act out, possibly to redirect a parent's anger from their partnering parent to themselves; perhaps to gain attention for someone to notice their need. Some children become invisible. These are just a few strategies, and every child and parent designs specific ways of "dancing" or relating. All of us have attachment strategies designed to help us be protected and comforted. In divorce, these strategies are not only activated in children but also in their parents. This is good to be aware of for adults too as they may have reactions based on their own attachment needs.

How does ongoing conflict impact children and their attachment relationships?

Conflict is hard on children, and they do poorly in family separation with enduring conflict. Children in these situations can end up with increased anxiety, depression, feelings of isolation, and relationship and emotional problems throughout life. Children who live with continuous conflict are more prone to behavioral problems. No parent wants this for their children, yet it is easy to let struggle, negativity, criticism, and blame towards a partnering parent overwhelm and overflow onto the child.

Another risk is a role reversal. It is easy for parents to enlist a child for support to get through these challenges, rather than getting support for their own struggles elsewhere so they can then meet the child's needs. It can have lifelong effects, putting a child at increased risk for relationship problems as adults, as they have learned that relationships may be unsafe.

In most cases, a child benefits from the presence and love of both of their parents. A child placed in between two warring parents faces consequences that are often devastating to their sense of security and development of self-worth. Research shows children do better by relating to both parents who do not ignore, but contain their conflict—two imperfect parents, who refuse to place the child between them in their dispute.

A family transition such as separation or divorce can threaten the child's sense of security as they are losing all that is "known" to them, what has been available to them and what they have designed strategies around. When conflict is high, they may also lose that sense of support from both parents, leaving them feeling alone. Isolation is the enemy in most circumstances. Divorce can be isolating for a child. Children may lose their sense of "community" as their family changes shape. In most cases this is remedied over time, however an awareness of the experience of the child will help reduce their isolation and strengthen their connections to family, friends and the community.

You defined attachment as the "relationship with a parent that provides safety, protection, and comfort." What do you mean by "protection?"

Before attachment is even possible, a person needs to experience safety, therefore safety and protection are foundational to attachment. Protection is more than eliminating hazards. With a foundation of attachment, a child needs protection from perceived danger and needs to have a firm sense of safety. In our context, think of *relational* safety and security. By saying this, I am not suggesting a parent is "unsafe" as we traditionally think of the word, or that a parent is doing anything to intentionally not protect their child. A parent reading this book is already working and involved precisely because they are intentional about helping their child know they are safe and loved.

I can see how divorce or separation may threaten a child's sense of security, or even seem dangerous. How does a child understand and react to this threat?

Change, the unknown, and loss are all inherent in separation and divorce. Any mammal has an instinctual physiologically driven reaction when faced with a threat. You have likely heard of the "fight, flight, freeze, and faint" reactions. Assessing danger happens on a physiological level. The body releases cortisol, adrenaline, and other chemicals preparing to react in the most appropriate way for survival. We are aware and can become hypervigilant when the environment cues us that there is a danger or threat. We are also unable to focus on much else when we feel threatened. For children, this can happen as they read very subtle cues—a change in the environment, facial or body language, or a sense of chaos or unpredictability. Again, this may not mean parents intend to increase stress. We may very well be working to prevent our child from knowing about the stress we are under, however, because our brains wire together through experiences, there is a shared truth in the situation we cannot deny. Things are stressful, and under stress, the emotional limbic system takes over and prepares for a response to the threat.

There are two responses to stress, called "mobilization", which mean we are getting ready to react: "fight or flight." To be "mobile" means to move freely. What is going on when a child is in "fight" mode? Anger, aggression, moving towards the threat to "slay" it rather than moving away, as in "flight." Our survival instinct tells us we must fight to the death. Outbursts, aggression, and even verbal arguments emerge.

What is happening when a child is in "flight" mode? A child is simply seeking to flee a threat, to get away, escape—avoiding people, seeking space, twisting out of a hug, etc. A baby may twist away or lean away from a parent. The limbic system has evaluated and assessed there is a threat, usually obvious but not always—remember the brain knows more than we can quickly cognitively understand, especially in crisis with contextual information flooding our senses. The brain in both of these cases is reacting to action, which occurs fast, with lightning speed coordination of systems and integration of information.

The remaining two reactions in crisis are what we call "immobilization" responses. In contrast to "mobilization", these two survival strategies are shutting down: "faint and freeze". They are the reduction of movement or "life" activities for a brief time.

"Freeze" is just that—playing statue, or having a "deer in the headlight" moment. It's as if any movement will shift the surrounding air, therefore, stillness provides protection. The child acts as if they are invisible. "Faint," on the other hand, is disassociation, checking out, sometimes even sleeping. Our body interprets the situation as a crisis, and it says, "This is not for me, but I can't get out fast enough, so let's check out." Children will resort to these without preplanning. They are instinctual responses.

In terms of survival, a feeling or sense of safety runs deeply. "Where do I live? Who will care for me? Who will protect me from predators (those who could do harm to a child)?" But safety also points to the deeper need for relational protection. "Will someone care about my feelings, provide me structure and predictability, and promote my agenda and joy?"

How can parents best create this sense of safety?

First, make sure you are seeing your child in the state they are in and meeting their developmental and relationship needs. Some children say straight up what they need; others are pleasers who want to keep peace, and may need help to state their feelings and needs clearly. Your child may have learned somewhere that they have to meet other people's needs, and may not have the skills to express their needs. Look them in the eye when they are not aware of your inquiry—what are their eyes telling you?

Further, we have two systems in our brains that can engage. The one described above reacts in a crisis, and there is another that is activated when experiencing safety and protection. This more calm state allows us to relate and process information and even plan for the future. In this calm state known as the *social engagement system*, a child is curious and creative; they can explore and can take in information. When we can foster the social engagement system, both parent and child are more relaxed, available to engage in the relationship, and problem solve. This is the state we want to foster in our children.

Your approach involves relational neuroscience, and you speak a lot about the brain. How is neuroscience part of this conversation?

We talked about the brain's capability to react when it perceives danger. Attachment also wires the brain as a parent and child react to one another. Do you know that when your child is born they have trillions of neurons, more than they will have at any other time in their lives? Since these neurons are unorganized and unconnected, every response we offer wires those connections. The brain wires around experience. Research has found that this process of wiring neural connections through experience happens at every age. This information is exciting, hopeful and daunting at the same time.

Another important aspect of our brains is considering the differences in the right and left hemispheres. In short, and broadly generalized, the right hemisphere helps us experience context, the senses, implicit information, and how a situation feels. The right hemisphere is fast; interpreting and assessing everything in the environment. The left hemisphere is slower to react, cognitively driven, more time oriented, and concerned with analyzing and planning. In situations of high stress or emotion, the right brain is in charge; so the wisdom of the left hemisphere is not yet welcomed. On the other hand, the left hemisphere may leave out contextual or emotional information, so both need to partner to integrate all of the available information.

Why is this important for parents?

Because parents need to understand where a child is in the course of processing information. They also can learn how to model, and help their child rely upon both important priorities of their brain and balance emotional and logical information.

Children who are enduring a family transition such as divorce are going through stress, trauma, and loss. They may be seeing their parents behave at their worst—embroiled in their own conflict and trauma. The brain wires around this experience and attachment strategies emerge in order to navigate these stresses. While the brain wiring around all the negative experiences may seem like bad news, the good news is the brain wires around positive experiences as well. There are always new opportunities to help your child cope and to repair when relational ruptures have occurred. Simply put, every experience has the chance to promote resiliency or adaptation to mitigate danger. One of the hardest parts of helping your child is watching them and allowing them to feel their true feelings of pain. I call this "necessary uncomfortableness."

> *"While the brain wiring around all the negative experiences may seem like bad news, the good news is the brain wires around positive experiences as well."*

In what way does "allowing necessary uncomfortableness" lead to increased resiliency for children?

No one wants to see their child in pain, especially pain that somehow is caused by the divorce. No matter how well supported a child is, how strong an attachment you have with your child, divorce causes them discomfort. Maybe the parent's relationship when they were together caused the child discomfort, especially if there was overt conflict. At any rate, the child will be affected by change. They may suffer. They should experience sadness and feel the loss. This is truth and it is their story. Parents should be cautious to only expose children to what they need to know about the conflict, but it would be false to pretend that the conflict doesn't exist. We want to be protective and comforting, but not rescue them from this "necessary uncomfortableness", because it is in enduring the struggle that resiliency is built. You know this as an adult – going through the valley has rewards of building strength and confidence. At your child's developmental level, this is the same. They can't dismiss or ignore the pain, and we don't really want them to. Rather, we want to help them go through it and learn how strong they are, and come out the other side more capable of handling life's adversity. This honesty is the first step to resiliency.

Promoting and Building Resiliency in Your Children

Is it possible to build resiliency in your child?

Absolutely, and the exciting part is that parents themselves can help their child navigate what is probably one of the most difficult passages they will encounter in their lives: a divorce. Counseling and other services can be helpful and in some cases essential. However, with Integrative Parent Coaching, the parent can be the most influential teacher and agent of change for their child. The parent's role is critical, as they have a unique ability to strengthen their reciprocal relationship and attachment, which helps both the parent and child build resilience.

What are some ways parents can help their child build resiliency?

It is not hard, but it does takes mindfulness and focus. It is easy to miss these opportunities to help your child grow in strength and coping abilities while navigating a family transition.

Don't miss the function of behavior. Avoid taking your child's mood, attitude, or behavior personally as they tell their story through their behavior. What are they trying to accomplish? What is their strategy? They need for you to be able to handle their pain, support them through it, and allow their other parent to help them through it.

Instead, step back, attune yourself to their feelings, and be with them in that place of discomfort. Allow your child to have their own experience of the family transition. You have your story, your perspective—honor theirs. I recognize it can be hard for parents who are going through stress themselves, but helping kids tell their story allows them to learn how to talk about their feelings and build resilience.

A significant benefit we may miss is that if a child is good at telling accurate stories about their life, the details of their day, etc., they are better able to protect themselves. They can get help if needed. If a child can tell their story with detail and accuracy, then they can tell someone if something is going wrong. Also, if there is a false story out there, they are better able to give an accurate report.

There are many strategies we can use to help a child recall, restore, and make meaning of their life stories in an integrated way. If a child does not want to talk about it, maybe they can draw a picture or build something out of Legos. It is important to give them the support to bring the inside stress out somehow.

Avoid overreacting. Keep the brain in mind. Because we can provide new experiences that wire the brain, we can help the child build resiliency, but only when we are safe and not over-reactive.

Imagine a child is very upset, emotional, "out of their mind" in a tantrum that, in our view, seems to have no reason. Get down to their level and connect to their emotions before trying to understand them. Children must learn how to handle their frustration and feelings, and they need parents to be co-regulators of their emotional state. Move toward, not away, especially when you are ready to discipline.

When your child misbehaves, is unkind, has an attitude, or simply has a moment of defiance, how do you know what to do next? It seems simple. "You discipline them, right?' Well, yes, no, maybe.

Discipline has at its root "to teach." Discipline as consequence and punishment without relating moves us away from this. Children need to understand structure and limits as this promotes safety—the core of everything we build on. However, consequences should follow a relational strategy of moving in towards the child through attuning and resonance.

Let's not forget that no matter what the struggle is in your family and your child's life, there are reasons in each developmental stage why a child may act out, push against authority, or try to assert their independence—this is normal, typical, and even healthy. It does not mean we do not react or have a game plan to help our child, but we can also relax. Parents have been dealing with this since the dawn of time. It happens in all families.

A two-year-old tests out his "no" muscle, which is useful for learning that he is separate and has autonomy, and which functions also as a safe structure in which to contain his anger. An eight-year-old hides her homework, possibly as an experiment to test what happens if she tries to skirt her responsibility. Wouldn't you rather she learn this now, instead of learning as a teen, when the consequences will be much greater? A teen rejects the plan to go to college to take a year-long road trip with his friends. You see the big picture view, the teen needs to assert his young adult independence.

All of these scenarios can be tough moments for parents. They can be even tougher if you and your partnering parent handle them differently. You care about your child and want to guide them in the best life for themselves. Sometimes when we feel challenged, our inability to remain calm and take another's point of view can escalate the situation and miss the target of increased relationship. When we react in a way that promotes the attunement and resonance between two brains in the relationship, as discussed earlier, your reaction will build relationship and trust. Practicing the skills of being present without an agenda, hearing their perspective, taking their perspective, reflecting, and acting to problem solve instills strength and confidence in a child's ability to navigate their world, at any age.

Don't leave your child guessing about boundaries. Teach boundaries; build fences with gates.

As your child develops, they learn more and more that they are separate from other people. This developmental understanding should be well in place before a child is 18 months old, but in some cases, the lines get blurred. As parents, we all want our children to be confident, assured, and exploring the world, while still knowing they are safe and have a soft place to fall. Remember, children are always looking for safety. Children need to be clear about what safety is, what it feels like, what behaviors promote safety, and who are the safe people.

Let's define what we are talking about: Boundaries are the limits we set in life that provide us autonomy (or independence), and authority over our space—knowing where you begin and I end. Boundaries allow your child to say, "I have authority to decide if it needs to change." Boundaries communicate, "This is where you end. I am separate, and that is a good thing." Fences are a good way to think about boundaries. Because we also want relationships to grow when they feel safe and allow for comfort, affection, and proximity, as well as social engagement, we can teach our children to add gates that they control to set limits on what makes them uncomfortable.

In divorce, children can get confused about these and may lose the strength of their fences and forget to open or close gates. Parents may rely on their child for their support and blur the boundary. It is vital that children see boundaries modeled for them by you, their parent, and by others in their life.

Protesting is good. I know that may seem like a bit of a provocative statement, however, we want our child to be able to say they disagree. It is also important that they are positively reinforced for making decisions to state and enforce their boundaries.

Say your child is at a family function, and Aunt Alice wants to enfold them in a kiss, but your child does not know Aunt Alice well or feel comfortable with her. Your child says "no." Well, that could hurt Aunt Alice's feelings. Other family members may pressure your child, "Oh, go on, and give her a hug." A simple statement such as, "Well, (my child) only feels comfortable hugging people they know really well. I'm sure you understand. Maybe a high five would be ok?" This way you have met the family pressure need, but not forced the child to be overly physical with someone they do not know well. You have also modeled for them healthy boundaries and a way to nicely say "no" and still stay in a relationship (although distant). Your child has increased confidence and the ability to manage these moments, even when you are not present. This is vital, as you will not always be present.

Boundaries are important for several reasons:

- *Boundaries provide the safety for children to develop.* When children do not have to worry about their safety, they can explore and engage themselves in curiosity. We know this can help in learning, gaining new skills, and socially and emotionally managing their world.

- *Boundaries protect your child.* Your child experiences two (or more) different social contexts, and these environments may differ. Maybe new partners or friends enter the picture. When parents can agree and collaborate when teaching about setting boundaries, the child is clear and can relax in the knowledge of assured safety in both homes and the broader world to some extent. When there is disagreement about where the gates are, who is allowed into personal space, or what the rules of social engagement are, then a child may feel they need to be more vigilant in their environment can take away from active exploration. I do not mean to frighten, but many children are violated or taught to engage too liberally with "family" (extended family or new affiliates of their parents), strangers, or acquaintances by being confused about boundaries. Children need to know they are in charge of their personal space.

They need to have their own sleep space and routines that help them calm down and get to sleep on their own, or with concrete plans that maintain boundaries.

- *Boundaries protect you.* When you create and model boundaries for your child, you teach them they have personal rights. In the process, you help protect your relationship with your child from unnecessary scrutiny.

Teach your child to talk about their boundaries, notice when they have set limits, and congratulate them. The previously mentioned skill of telling their story will make it easier for them to tell you when/if something goes wrong with boundaries, or if they ever feel uncomfortable with someone in their life.

Don't ask your child to separate their experiences into two worlds. Work to offer them one unified body of experience.

A common theme when children have two households is that they feel they cannot share their experiences from one home with their other parent. Parents send messages either explicitly—"I don't want to hear about your time with your dad"— or subtly and implicitly through body language and facial expression. Children read these messages loud and clear. If parents stop and think about their child's world, however, do they want to ask a child to have two worlds of experience? One that leaves out a big part of who they are and their life story?

In most cases, it is best for your child to allow them, and even encourage them, to share about their time with the other parent. It is helpful if a parent can send supportive messages like, "I am glad you had fun at the beach with your mom" or "Your dad is really good at helping with homework—I am happy you worked on your math together." I call these "joining statements". They tell the child they are allowed to integrate their life, and they help to increase your child's attachment to you as a parent because they can share their full self.

"A common theme when children have two households is that they feel they cannot share their experiences from one household with their other parent. Parents send messages either explicitly—"I don't want to hear about your time with your dad"— or subtly and implicitly through body language and facial expression."

Don't let your child become isolated. Surround them with a caring community.

Just as you may be adjusting to the loss of friends or a sense of community, your child may also be encountering these kinds of adjustments. Everything they have known has changed as well. Belonging to a larger community can provide support and help ease the discomfort of adjusting to divorce or a loss of any kind. Isolation is never a good thing. In fact, isolation is the enemy in most cases. Think about it for a moment: If we are isolated, we only have our perspective. We cannot comfort ourselves well. We are not able to create new skills or ways of being that improve our situation. And, we cannot get input as we move forward.

Let's be clear, it is fine to be alone sometimes. Isolation is a deeper state of aloneness. The difference is whether or not we have resources outside of ourselves. The danger in complex situations is that isolation may grow and further embed us into thinking we have no support. Children are aware of the pain their parents are in and sometimes also have an awareness of their own pain. Isolation may increase in cases where parents are not able to meet their child's needs or when the child is attempting to meet the parent's need, which can be an unhealthy role reversal. In other complex situations, a partnering parent may hinder a child's acceptance and level of comfort in their new community, or in the same community with the other parent.

In any case, your child needs to expand their community and have a sense of belonging to a "place" that bonds them to you. They need to know they are part of a larger community, family, circle of support, and friends. This belonging promotes healthy adjustment for them by creating stability. You may need to stretch outside of your comfort zone a bit, but it will be well worth the effort.

Think about your community. What is it based upon? Shared interests with others? Being close in proximity? Working towards shared values and goals? Now think of your son or daughter. Their world is no doubt smaller, as it should be, but the questions are the same. Does your child have a place to be with other children or individuals who share their interests— say activities such as sports, art, or hobby clubs? Do they know the parks, landmarks, and fun places near your home and in your community? If you no longer live in the same town or area you lived in together before the divorce or separation, this is especially important.

Being involved locally will help your child understand their sense of belonging, which is helpful in all cases of family transition and is especially important where there is complexity in your family. All of these become anchors to create resiliency in the experience and relationship you have with your child.

Tips for increasing community anchors:

- Sign your child up for activities they find interesting.

- Visit local parks and point out to your child the features they can remember, "This is the castle park, this is the park with the big slide, etc." Point the park out as you pass by it while driving. You want the child to be able to "mark" the landscape in the community.

- Visit local history and cultural landmarks in your community. Read books or create stories to go with them.

- Have your child draw a map each week adding a place you have visited and keep the art in a place they can see and review.

- For older children, have a treasure hunt in the community to explore and investigate the area.

- Remember, nature builds brains, so get outside and have your child enjoy whatever landscape is around.

Don't ignore your own work. While children do not need to know everything about your conflict with your partnering parent, depending on their age, allowing them to know how you handle difficulties will both normalize the situation and give them skills for navigating their struggles. Allow that "necessary uncomfortableness". Model how to manage adversity and fix ruptures. Refuse to put your child in the middle. Discouraging time with their other parent puts the child squarely in the middle of the conflict.

> ***"Refuse to put your child in the middle. Discouraging time with their other parent puts the child squarely in the middle of the conflict."***

Why is it important for a child to be able to tell their own story?

We all need to make sense of our experiences. We all relate stories of our lives daily. It helps us know who we are in the world and what difference we make. That is why the world is filled with stories. Commercials, songs, people's conversation, and of course, literature, history, science, etc. Stories help us remember and understand. They clarify and give meaning. We all need stories and children are no different.

Regardless of the age of your child, they have a story to tell. It is now, and will be in the future, their own story, with many chapters. The younger they are, the less likely it is that they can narrate the experiences in their life that are chapters of this story. Early on in childhood, memory is stored in a way we refer to as implicit, which means they store memories in senses, feelings, and images without language. Implicit memory is always attached to a larger sense of how things felt, "how" the experience was for them. As children develop, they can start wrapping language around their experiences. You may find they share specifics about their days and experiences with increased details. It is normal for children to sometimes embellish the details and "tell a tale." Not to worry, as this is typical and children usually outgrow it. Paying attention to their daily chapters will help your child tell an accurate story of their lives. At the same time that they narrate the details of their day, we want to see the child increase their ability to talk about their own feelings. The brain integrates and wires around these skills, building on them throughout their life.

We know that children who can tell their stories benefit in many ways. First, being able to put words to feeling states, even at a young age, helps children be more resilient, cope better in difficult situations, and get support and help when they need it. The child is better able to regulate or manage their emotions. Anytime we can wrap language around our experiences, we have more mastery over our emotions and are better able to manage stress.

> *"Anytime we can wrap language around our experiences, we have more mastery over our emotions and are better able to manage stress."*

Secondly, a child who shares their story can build meaning from their experiences rather than something they merely hear, or someone told them. Of course, they can take input, but they can also recall their implicit and explicit experiences and hold that meaning.

In some cases, a child may be in a circumstance where a parent does not support their fully integrated perspective of their story, meaning what they have experienced in their life. In divorce, especially when there is conflict, a child may not be fully able to hold two experiences of belonging in both of their homes to an equal degree due to the lack of a parent's support or receiving a negative message. For example, let's say a partnering parent talks as if you were not around when the child was young. The child asserts this and firmly believes it—you were not around or helping when they were a baby, which can be confusing for the child who remembers implicit knowledge of their experience, even before they have language for it. A parent can react with lots of emotion and defensiveness, but our anger does not help the child build resilience.

So what is a parent to do? Rather than argue, which only increases the negative stress chemicals in the brain, we let the child state their point and reflect the statement by acknowledging the child's underlying need. A parent might say, "You're worried I wasn't around. I would have missed you so much if I had not been around. That would be sad for you and me." Showing a child a picture of themselves at that age, with you or where you know the story, and asking them to talk about the picture will help them build neural connections around the facts, and help them understand you were truly there. No interviewing, lecturing, or forcing them to recall—just giving them a chance to integrate their story, given new information. This does not mean that the child has to argue with the other parent, it just means they have an alternative narrative they can recall.

Although having both parents care enough to put the child first is optimal, one parent can make a difference and teach the child how to integrate both of their home experiences. Remember, it is more important to help your child develop their story than to allow them to create a story that omits significant chapters from their experience. It strengthens your relationship with them when you encourage them to embrace their whole life experience.

In closing, what is one meaningful thing a parent can do today to support their children?

You've read this far, so you have already done something meaningful for your children. Congratulate yourself for that. Regarding doing something with your child, children love novelty, so try something new: surprise them! Play, dance, explore your world, read together, create art, or cook something new together. Look into your child's eyes and tell them without words how valuable they are and how much their story means to you. Most importantly, today and every day, be with them fully; in person, on the phone, or in spirit.

> *"Look into your child's eyes and tell them without words how valuable they are and how much their story means to you."*

Integrative Parent Coaching is developed to provide meaningful ideas for parents to enhance their relationship with their child and help promote their child's resiliency. I would be happy to discuss these concepts further, and I encourage you to visit my website at www.integrativeparentcoaching.net or my Facebook page: "Kristine Clay Integrative Parent Coaching." I have a blog, and I offer parent coaching, consultation, and other support to any geographic location. My best to you as you support your child through the journey of a family transition.

References:

Cozolino, L. (2014). *The neuroscience of human relationships: Attachment and the developing social brain.* New York: Norton.

Crittenden, P. (2008). *Raising parents: attachment, parenting and child safety.* Cullompton: Willan Publications.

Porges, S. (2011). *The polyvagal theory: Neurophysiological foundations of emotions, attachment, communication, and self-regulation.* New York: W. W. Norton.

Siegel, D. (2013). *Brainstorm: The power and purpose of the teenage brain.* New York, New York: Tarcher/Penguin.

Siegel, D. (2012). *Pocket guide to interpersonal neurobiology*. New York, NY: Norton.

ABOUT KRISTINE CLAY, MA

As the developer of "integrative parent coaching", Kristine Clay works closely with parents to be an effective agent of change and healing for their child and family through the difficult changes in divorce or complex custody situations. Kristine brings her passion and knowledge to her practice and guides parents in rebuilding and/or strengthening their relationship with a child – or children – of any age who may have faced challenges as their family changed. Kristine brings over 25 years of experience working with families in crisis, trauma or those simply struggling with the demands of life. She has been involved in the community as a teacher, therapist, and supervisor for programs that support families. Her work has progressed to work specifically with families navigating complex custody, high conflict divorce, parental alienation or with families where a parent's influence and relationship with their child has in some way been compromised. She believes every child deserves to have the love and care of an interested parent.

Integrative Parent Coaching is not typical parent skills training but specialized strategies for using neuroscience and attachment or relationship building skills to repair and strengthen connections. Both focuses bring much-needed hope to strengthening relationship as the brain wires around experience every day. Her favorite quote is "Healing happens in the present," as every single relational interaction has the potential for repairing hurting parents and children. Consultation, coaching or any support can be done in person or long distance through phone and skype options.

Kristine did undergraduate studies at the University of Washington and graduate work at Gonzaga University. She is a PsyD candidate in psychology at California Southern University where she pursues a Doctorate in Psychology. In her doctoral work, she focuses on interpersonal neurobiology, attachment, trauma, family systems, complex custody and divorce.

BUSINESS: Integrative Parent Coaching, LLC

WEBSITE: www.integrativeparentcoaching.net

EMAIL: kristine@kristineclay.com

PHONE: 360.265.1254

LOCATION: Greater Seattle area, WA

FACEBOOK: www.facebook.com/kristineclayparentcoaching/

LINKEDIN: www.linkedin.com/pulse/beyond-typical-parenting

CHAPTER SEVEN

How to Establish Boundaries and Promote Healthy Communication

by Maida V. Farrar

Your ex is not your child's ex.

With over a decade of experience as a family law attorney in California, Maida witnessed first-hand how inherently destructive divorce can be to families. After observing the anguish and heartache many families go through, Maida shifted her focus to helping families navigate transitions in life through coaching and mediation. She employs empathy and compassion with each of her clients to help them achieve confidence, clarity, and outcomes that put children first while supporting the needs and emotional health of all those involved.

Maida sums up her approach: "My general philosophy is that I want my clients to be able to get through the divorce process with minimal conflict. I think the foundation of that is in communication. I want them to be able to communicate as best they can under the circumstances and to understand that it is 'under the circumstances'. I want them to be able to say what they need to say to each other and to hear what is being said without being triggered by that process. I want them to be able to set and maintain boundaries because once they can get to that point, being able to maintain those boundaries means freedom."

Having informally coached her clients for years while working as a divorce lawyer, Maida has found that her current role as a Life Coach and Certified Divorce Coach aligns with her passion for helping people navigate the divorce process with as little conflict as possible. She helps her clients make informed decisions about the divorce process, set and maintain healthy boundaries, manage their emotions, set goals, create a workable action plan to achieve those goals, and find a balance between the legal process and moving on with their lives.

> *"I try to approach divorce by taking a step back from Family Law...It provides my clients an opportunity to take a step back from Family Law, as well, and all of the baggage that comes with that title."*

It's important to Maida that parents are able to regain control and confidence through this process, so they feel secure in their future and know their children won't suffer. She's been successful helping her clients through the overwhelming process of divorce and separation by easing much of the negative impact that divorce may have, enabling her clients to move forward with confidence.

Maida offers a wide range of coaching services, from individual coaching to group coaching, to seminars and other events. She also and speaks to groups about the importance of setting boundaries, improved communication, and achieving optimal results while navigating divorce and separation.

In this chapter, Maida draws from her experience as a family law attorney, divorce coach, and mediator to share her advice on:

- The realities of divorce, family court, and mediation

- How to stay goal focused by starting with the end in mind

- The most common misconceptions parents have about divorce and family court

- How to communicate effectively, diffuse conflict, and solve problems even when your ex is "high conflict" or narcissistic

- How to establish boundaries that reduce conflict

- How to communicate with your children and be sensitive to their emotional needs

- How to create your support network

Meet Maida

Jeremy: Maida, you have a really interesting background. You started in family court as an attorney, but over the years, you evolved your practice to focus more on coaching and mediation. Can you share a little bit about your background and how you got into this field?

Maida: A little over ten years ago, I began practicing law in California exclusively in the family law arena. Over time, I became more and more frustrated, really more with the system than anything else, and started looking into alternatives for my clients to be able to get through family law processes—whether it's a divorce or modifications to custody issues. Mediation and coaching were a natural progression and addition to my practice.

I'm also a Certified Divorce Coach, in that role, I help my clients navigate the divorce process. I want them to have as little conflict as possible when they're going through this process. My background as an attorney lets me help my clients make more informed decisions.

A lot of what we work on is setting healthy boundaries, working on communication strategies, and laying the foundation so that they can have a better experience through that process.

When you say "frustration with the system," was your issue with the participants in the system or how the system works?

Both the system and the participants in the system. When I think of the participants, I'm actually thinking of the litigants who are at odds with one another.

Was there a defining moment, a series of events, or just a change of heart that inspired you to do this work? I know your perspective is more about helping parents navigate the process and come to reasonable solutions that put children first, rather than having them deal with the adversarial process of the family court system. Can you expound on your inspiration to get into this work?

There were several defining moments, I would say four to five years ago when I began to shift the directions in which I was headed. I had a handful of pretty high-conflict cases; neither side could get any resolution through the court system so the case couldn't move forward.

Often you may have high-conflict parents who have so much emotion involved that there is an active irrationality on their part. In this particular example, there was one stage where we had two attorneys trying to get them through this process, and it just wouldn't work. There was no decision making on the part of the court to even give these highly emotional parties something to hold onto, so they were in constant limbo for probably 3 years. I think this was really devastating to the children.

Right, and, both the parents and children lost three years of resolution. And, unfortunately, three years isn't uncommon. I often hear of five, even eight years.

Absolutely. I had another case where the divorce was very easy, but the aftermath was years of litigation. It really depends on a number of factors, including the parties' and their willingness to try to settle things, too.

What are some of the most common obstacles parents and your clients run into, and how do you help them overcome these obstacles?

I think the most common obstacle is that parents can get in their own way by maintaining preconceived notions about how a particular communication exchange is going to go. For example, "Oh, I can't talk to my ex about that because he/she will just say this," or, "I can't do that because I already know this is going to happen." I work with them to get around that tunnel vision and to explore other outcomes. One of the ways I do this is to get the client to begin with the end in mind.

I believe there're three categories most negative communications in family law, divorce, and separation can be reduced to: communications that are blaming, communications which are demanding, and communications which are diagnosing. A "blaming" communication may look like: "This is all your fault." or "Well, I can't do this because he/she always does that." It's assuming they aren't able to do something and then assigning fault as to why. Communications that are "demanding" are pretty easy for most people to come up with. "Diagnosing" communications may look like "I can't negotiate with crazy." or "My ex is bipolar."

It seems, "starting with the end in mind," may be harder in practice, especially when we're in the middle of the process. The divorce may still be very heated and there may be a lot of anger and resentment.

How do you help facilitate healthy communication and get the parents to keep the end in mind? How do you help them see their current behaviors and current actions are not aligned with their goals?

It all depends. For some people, the conflict is so high that the end that we're talking about might very well be the end of the hour. It really can be reduced to, "What is it going to take for us to get through this meeting," for example. "What is it going to take for us to get through x?" When I'm with an individual client, it might be, "What is it going to take to get through the holidays?" It really depends on the situation and ideally, if the parties are working with me as a mediator, they can both communicate with me what kind of outcome it is that they're looking for. Mediation requires that there is some buy-in from both of the parties, that this is the process they want to use.

With individual clients, I assume they want to reach a different outcome than what they're used to. We explore what alternatives might look like. If we're going down a road that looks negative, we might explore in the abstract a little bit because they can both see, "This is not going to turn out well. Nothing good comes from continuing to attack one another because we can't get to the goal that we've set. What's one thing we can do differently?" We start there.

Straight Facts: The Realities of Divorce, Family Court, and Mediation

What are some of the most common misconceptions parents have about divorce in general and also with the family court process?

I think probably one of the most common misconceptions about divorce, in general, is the time frame. Some people have this idea that it can be done quickly.

Another common misconception is that you must have an attorney. If you look at the statistics, most people don't have an attorney, but people often think that if you have an attorney, the outcome of the divorce will be "fair". I think what's "fair" and what's "equitable" are very different things. These aren't concepts people generally think about. You might ask somebody, "Why do you want it this way?" They respond, "Well, because it's fair." I think that that's really where our misconception is—that we're going to go through this process and, in the end, it's going to come out and it's going to be "fair". I try to steer people away from that word.

"Fair" is a very subjective term, because what's "fair" to me may not be "fair" to you.

Right, but people commonly say, "I want this because this is what's fair." That can be a real attachment and it gets thrown around a lot. That's really why I try to get people away from that word because life's not fair.

You mentioned that you don't necessarily have to have an attorney, but let's say the other parent does have an attorney. Most people aren't experts in the law. How does one go through the process if they don't have an attorney?

I would say that's really up to the individual. There's a common belief that if one person has an attorney, that the other person should "lawyer up." But if going that route is not really what that particular person wants to do, then I don't think they should. There might be a better use of their money elsewhere.

> *"There's a common belief that if one person has an attorney, that the other person should 'lawyer up'. But if going that route is not really what that particular person wants to do, then I don't think they should. "*

Other times, I would say it really depends on the other party and the attorney they've hired. Have they hired an attorney that really is going to litigate the case? Then you may want to do yourself a favor and hire one as well. I think it's really situational for people. At the same time, it's important to interview more than one attorney to make sure they're a good fit for you. If you really want to pursue settlement and you hire somebody who wants to take you to court immediately, that's not a good fit.

It's really identifying number one, "What would I like to get out of this process?" Then, number two, "Is there someone out there that can help me with that?"

Let's say you're in a situation where one of the parties is higher-conflict or there's a power imbalance, one party always has to have their way, but the other party doesn't want to "lawyer up", as you say. This parent wants to pursue mediation or even co-parenting counseling because they really just want a peaceful resolution. If the other parent is unwilling to contribute financially towards the mediation, do you think it's a good idea or bad idea to offer to pay for all of the mediation or counseling? Are there any disadvantages to them paying for all the mediation?

I don't necessarily see any practical disadvantages to that, but it really depends on the parties. If you have one person who is really not going to be invested in the mediation process, you may want to ask yourself if that's money well spent.

Good point. Are there any alternative strategies one can pursue? Perhaps they've tried the court-appointed mediator, but it didn't work because that person wasn't necessarily particularly skilled in mediating divorces in which one party is unwilling to compromise, or perhaps the mediator was just overloaded. What do you recommend?

There are alternative strategies, but anytime you're getting into mediation, or even into the collaborative model, as I mentioned before, it does require some kind of buy-in from both parties. What if one party's willing to pay for it? Again, I don't see any practical problem with that. However, there is also that theory out there that if someone else is paying for it for you, then you don't value it.

There are alternatives to a litigated divorce, and I think those alternatives get overlooked largely because people are afraid. However, too often people think, "I'm getting a divorce. I need to talk to an attorney." This concept is ingrained in us.

Right, this is the narrative we're brought up with. Reflexively, the first thing people do is call the attorney rather than seeking lower-conflict, more therapeutic, and reconciliatory alternatives. Would you suggest for people to hire a coach first? What process would you recommend?

If papers have already been filed, there might be some value in at least talking to an attorney, just to see what the structural outline of the divorce process is. That doesn't necessarily mean you will find yourself in a litigated divorce. I think working with someone like a coach at the outset to hone in on what your goals are for the process is incredibly valuable. This may help flesh out your ultimate goals and vision for what a low, or lower, conflict divorce process might look like.

> *"I think working with someone like a coach at the outset to home in on what your goals are for the process is incredibly valuable. This may help flesh out your ultimate goals and vision for what a low, or lower, conflict divorce process might look like."*

"Look, I really don't want to go to court. I really don't. I want to find a way to settle this." Having that conversation could lay the foundation for the kind of professionals you then seek out. Then, instead of going to talk to an attorney, you go talk to a mediator. A good mediator will tell you whether or not mediation seems like an appropriate path for you and your spouse. If you have a mediator that says, "Okay, here's my retainer. This will get you maybe 10 hours. Call your ex," that's not somebody I would want to hire. Regardless of whether you hire an attorney, a coach, or a mediator, you still want to make sure that whoever you're hiring is a good fit for you.

How to Communicate Effectively, Diffuse Conflict, and Solve Problems

Given that you focus on communication strategies, what are some of the symptoms of say, poor communication?

There are often literally physical symptoms people will display. For example, they may get tunnel vision, then get tense. Some people can recognize their heart rate is elevated, and they may begin to act defensively. They may belittle or shame the other person. In divorce, it's common to pull up past history. They may even shut down and then not feel like they're able to say what they want to say.

Can you expound a little bit on some specific ways that communication breaks down in a divorce or separation, and how it can be avoided?

Communication tends to break down because there are so many emotions involved and problems that led to issues in the marriage resurface. These problems don't just go away because someone filed for divorce. They often continue through the divorce process, so it can be very difficult to avoid negative communication. I think that at that point in time, the other person needs to focus on, "What am I going to do to shore myself up against that?"

If you engage with someone that's going to make it worse, it will spiral downward from there. That's where, I believe, really, disengagement comes into play and the need to set up boundaries becomes, even more, important.

Many parents may have poor communication skills, but they may not necessarily be adversarial. How do you help these clients?

Mediation is really about getting clients through that hour; having them identify a goal at the beginning of the session and then getting them to try to reach that goal. This might be, "Okay, at the end of this session, what we want to be able to do is have a strategy for when we're going to put the house on the market and what needs to be done in order to do that." If things are going very, very poorly, or if I'm working with an individual client whose partner may have a narcissistic personality disorder, then we'll work on techniques for disengagement. Ultimately, I try to help them find a strength that they can focus on.

How do you deal with situations where one person is conflict-avoidant and the other person is more high-conflict? For example, if the conflict-avoidant person perhaps isn't as good at communicating, because they associate it with conflict and the other person communicates, but in an adversarial way.

In those situations, I generally try to move the clients away from the specific event or the piece that's triggering either the shut down on one side or the wanting to poke the bear by the other. There's a piece we draw from Marshall Rosenberg's "Nonviolent Communication", where I try to identify what the underlying needs are in that moment. For example, the person who may be poking the bear and being really high-conflict, what they might need is to be heard, so they're doing everything they can to talk, to be loud, to talk over. You can say, "You want to be heard. Okay, well we're going to give you the opportunity." The person who is conflict-avoidant, their underlying need may be to be respected in that moment, and they feel like they're being attacked. We can, again, if parties are open to it, cut these things down to really identify what's going on underneath the surface.

How do you do that with somebody that has narcissistic or borderline personality disorder, particularly if they don't even know they have it?

It really depends, and this walks a very fine line of diagnosing, but nevertheless, in family law, we come up against these issues. Even If someone hasn't been diagnosed with narcissistic personality disorder, they very well may display traits of a narcissist. Just because someone hasn't been diagnosed doesn't mean that we're still not dealing with the behavioral traits of it.

When you're dealing with someone like that, I have found the best way to work with it is to have my clients deal with them as little as possible. That may come down to controlling the variables, such as setting up an email account that is only for this person to use and which you only check between 7-7:30 PM. It's important to establish strict boundaries so you can be protected as much as possible, and this comes back to being able to communicate under the circumstances. You really need to understand and know that the other person is not going to change.

I think that's a great idea. It can help you in a couple of different ways. First, compartmentalizing and separating those communications, because you could receive an email that just ruins your day due to something he or she says. Then also, to be able to create that boundary of space, "Okay, this email is just for my correspondence, so I'm going to be in the right frame of mind when I'm reading it so that it won't impact me and it won't ruin my mood for the rest of the day. "It makes communication with that other person a little easier.

It might also be saying, "I'm only going to check my email between 7-7:30 PM and then I'm not going to respond to this email until tomorrow after I've had my coffee." Then there's not that emotional reaction to it. Create a barrier between you and the other person, but make sure you're respecting that barrier, too.

I think a great rule to have, too, is if you have an email that triggers an emotional response, don't respond immediately. Or, write the email, but employ the 24-hour rule. Go back to it and discard most of it. At least, you've vented—for your peace of mind—then you can formulate what Bill Eddy terms a BIFF response: brief, informative, friendly, and firm.

Sure, and it takes practice. It's not something I can simply tell someone to do and then they immediately can. It's not an easy thing to do. Often, you get a nasty email, or what I like to call nasty-grams. Usually, there are 1-2 pieces of important information in the email surrounded by 10-12 antagonistic items: name calling, trying to get the other person to justify something, et cetera. It's about being able to parse out, "Which part of this email do I really need to respond to, if anything?"

Can you speak to communication strategies, not just with the other parent, but with your children? What are some guidelines parents should adhere to when it comes communicating with their children?

I think communication strategies with your children, number one, should be age-appropriate. Even more importantly, parents should understand you're setting an expectation for your children by the way you communicate with them, and by the way you communicate with the other parent. There's a balance there. It's important for parents to allow children to be able to have their own emotions surrounding the divorce or separation, even when those emotions may conflict with the parents. Allow your children to express anger with Mom or Dad in a healthy, constructive manner. But, don't allow communication to become destructive. It boils down to creating a safe space for your children to have emotions and express themselves, and if it gets really heightened, don't hesitate to have your child see a counselor who can provide a neutral space to process their emotions.

> *"It's important for parents to allow children to be able to have their own emotions surrounding the divorce or separation, even when those emotions may conflict with the parents. Allow your children to express anger with Mom or Dad in a healthy, constructive manner."*

Clearly children will have a lot of different emotions going on. How important is it for parents to let their children know it's okay to have these emotions? That they can have feelings of anger or sadness, that it's okay for them to express these feelings with the parent so they don't feel silenced or invisible, and to ensure that their emotions don't manifest into destructive behaviors?

I think giving your child space to be able to have these emotions is probably one of the most important things a parent can do because it allows the child to move through the process as well. Your children are going through their own process with the divorce and it looks a lot different for them than it does for Mom or Dad, but they need to be able to move through that process, too, so they can get to the other side.

Establish Boundaries to Reduce Conflict

What are boundaries and why are they necessary in divorce or separation?

Boundaries—at a very basic level—would be, "I'm separate from you." Easier said than done. The way I like to look at boundaries in the context of divorce and separation is, "'We' no longer negatively impacts 'Me'." That's the goal of a boundary in divorce or separation. It's really easy to say, "Yeah, I'm separate from you. Okay, I've got that." In the context of divorce, there's probably a lot of enmeshment, but it's "we" because there still is the "we" there as you're going through the divorce or separation process. But, it's no longer going to negatively impact "me".

Right. There's a relationship that exists beyond the divorce because you're forever intertwined if you have children together.

Exactly, and you really can't get around that, you really can't—but you can learn to make it work. I think people can learn to work with it differently and the parents who are successful will do just that. Sometimes, it just takes time.

What are the top 3 boundaries that parents should establish? I imagine it's unique in each situation, but are there some universal boundaries?

I think a universal one that I work with people on, and it's unique to today's world, is to stay out of each other's lives. For a lot of people, that translates to "no Facebook stalking." You don't need to see what the other person is doing. You really, really don't. This is something that can be a trigger for someone, I think as a general rule, just staying out of each other's lives is probably one of the most important boundaries to institute.

Working on respectful communication is another big one. Not everyone needs to do the business-like conversations, although sometimes it's a good place to start.

Not involving children in adult conversations is a huge one and some parents are really good at that. Sometimes, they're really good at shielding their kids from the process, or making sure that whatever exposure the children have to the process is age-appropriate and is coming from both parents, from a place of love for the children.

Again, a lot of these boundaries are situational. I mentioned communicating only during certain times before. Also communicating in writing can be helpful. This goes back to staying out of each other's lives. You're not this other person's wife or husband anymore, so stop acting like it. You don't have to take care of this for them. They're an adult.

Right, or using children as messengers or spies, for example, "What's daddy's girlfriend like?" "What's mommy's boyfriend like?" Things like that.

Yes, those are questions that are not appropriate to ask the kids. Sometimes kids will offer up information like, "Hey, daddy's got a new girlfriend." It's really up to the parent at that point in time not to perpetuate that conversation. A response to that might be, "You know what? It's really great that your father's happy. Let's go see what's for dinner."

That's a good point, too, in terms of the response from the parent. Many people might be unsure how to deal with that situation. You don't want to communicate a negative response, but at the same time, you have feelings that haven't been reconciled yet. Just as you said, it's probably in the best interest of the child to say, "Oh, that's great. I'm happy for him." I guess there're various boundaries that need to be established. When should they be set, exactly?

Early and often.

Early and often and revisited?

Yes. I think they should be set early because it's a whole lot easier to expand a boundary than it is to contract it and make it more restrictive over time. The sooner the boundaries are set, the more opportunities my clients get to practice them because it isn't something that you just do once and it's done. It's something you will do over and over and over again, so early is better. People find that if they step in earlier, it becomes easier, faster.

It's one thing to set the boundaries in your own head or set boundaries by court order, but what do you think is the best way to establish these boundaries?

When I'm looking at the individuals in mediation and we get into, "This is what I need. I need to be heard. I need to be respected," we then structure some agreed-upon boundaries. It may be something like, "Mom is going to email Dad on Tuesday about X, Y, and Z, and Dad is going to email Mom on Friday about X, Y, and Z about the kids." We establish that there is an expectation that our communications serve to keep each other informed about what's going on with the kids, but that we're going to get everyone into a structure so the parties can then facilitate the work of dissolving ties to one another while still being parents for the children.

That makes perfect sense, but of course, with kids, life happens. Life has a way of getting in the way of maintaining perfect adherence to agreements. So can boundaries be flexible? You mentioned they can be revisited. Can you discuss that a little bit?

I believe boundaries have the ability to become flexible because life does happen and when we run across people who are rigid, that doesn't usually wind up working well. When you have some flexibility, it allows the boundary to stay in place. Again, this is a function of how well the parties are working together or communicating.

Does that expand to, let's say, parenting plans, too? For example, the time we return the kids—within reason. "I'm supposed to return our kids at 3 PM and well, we're running a little bit late, so it's going to be 3:15. Is that okay?" We don't want such rigidity like, "Nope, it's got to be 3:00. We didn't agree upon 3:15."

"It's 3:05, I'm calling the cops." I'm kidding, by the way.

Right. Exactly.

Calling about the drop-off being late over 15 minutes is good for the kids. A situation like that where someone's like, "No, it's 3:00," that's really more about control—that person is trying to exercise control over the other person. Absent any other information, that would be my gut-level response. In that situation, it is not about the boundary, it's about trying to make sure that someone else does what you want them to do.

Right, it's about one parent asserting power or control.

Of course, if you have somebody who is perpetually 20-30 minutes late, and maybe they don't call or they want you to change your schedule to accommodate them, that is a different situation. Under these circumstances, saying, "No, it needs to be 3:00," would be maintaining needed boundaries. It's about context. Every family is different.

Right, basically you're saying if it's an ongoing thing and that parent is perpetually late, perpetually a half hour, an hour late, not calling,

that's a pattern. It's not a unique situation. That is definitely a different circumstance, and it may make sense to more vigilantly enforce established agreements.

What are some other areas for healthy boundaries and what is a common objection you get from parents?

I think the biggest objection I run across with people is that it's hard, that it can initially create some discomfort, that the other party doesn't respect them. Honestly, setting up boundaries, in the beginning, can be hard and often times when you set a boundary, other people around you, whether it's your ex or your friends, they may not react well. Sometimes, they can be a bit put off by it, so it can be a tricky place to be in. That's why I say it really does require practice in order to be able to do it effectively. We naturally want to connect with people, and setting boundaries can cut into that a little bit. We're social beings. We want to do things for one another. It's natural to who we are as humans.

Maida, you mentioned in a previous conversation that you have a five-step process you employ to help parents establish boundaries. Can you briefly summarize what that five-step process is?

In my view, the process to establish and set boundaries is about cutting the emotional ties that didn't work, so parents can build things that do work for them as individuals. My process is as follows:

> **Step 1 - Seek to Accept & Understand:** The traditional first step is to accept and understand that you are on a new path. Accept that the "new normal" starts now. So, what are acceptance and understanding? At its essence, they are our ability to ascend to a position where we recognize the reality of our situation, we recognize the situation may be uncomfortable--even negative--but

we understand we can't, nor should we try to change, protest or abandon the situation.

Step 2 - Get Support: Next, as a parent, you should be aware how important it is to have support through the process because it's too hard to try to do everything alone. To join a support group and work with a professional can do wonders. Most important, a support group and a professional (such as a divorce coach or therapist) will help you navigate your divorce, heal faster and emerge stronger.

Step 3 - Communicate Effectively: Third, healthy communication is key. I work with clients on how to know themselves. To develop self-awareness and better know yourself is a critical part of the process. I help clients learn what really works for them and the other party, and what doesn't work and employ these lessons in how they communicate with the other parent. Poor communication is at the heart of marital breakdown and it can be the leading cause of conflict in divorce.

Step 4 - Fourth, once you learn what works for you--great!--you're on the right path. At the start, you may need to make new rules around the things that work, and stop using anything that doesn't work (or elevates conflict). This is where the rubber meets the road because you're taking back some of your own self-control.

Step 5 - Accept The Fact Your Ex Is Not Your Responsibility: Finally, once you arrive at a place where you understand and accept that your ex is no longer your responsibility, you will feel a tremendous release, as if a burden has been lifted. This is a positive step forward that will aid your healing and recovery process.

Also, it's important to learn your co-parent's triggers. You are likely already aware of many of your former spouse's triggers, but it's important to keep those triggers top of mind and be conscious of how they may have evolved through the divorce. Likewise, as this is an ongoing process, continue to learn to identify your triggers and develop strategies on how not to feed into them.

> **Bonus Step 6 - Protect Your Kids**: Now the bonus, and I can't say enough about this. Leave your kids out of it! Kids need the time and space to be kids. Insulate them from divorce issues, any conflict that arises, and anything that should be reserved for adult discussions.

How to Create Your Support Network

Clearly, having a support system is extremely important, but what exactly defines a support system? For example, about a year after his separation, a friend of mine got into a new relationship. His new partner was very supportive, but at the same time, it created significant stress on the relationship and ultimately the relationship did not work out.

Can you talk about what a support network looks like? I think even with friends, certain friends don't want to always hear everything that's going wrong in your divorce or all of your challenges and struggles. They're empathetic towards it, but it comes to a point where there's probably other support people that you should rely on, like a professional coach. How do you build that support network? What does that look like?

I would say at the outset that a new significant other probably wouldn't fall under my idea of a support system, at least in this context, because as you said, that brings its own set of complications. I would say it could be a part of a larger support network. Friends are great, but also understanding that your friends and your social circle are often also "going through the divorce" with you, too. They're figuring out who gets custody of the friends. Sometimes it's obvious, sometimes it's not. Often there are support groups in your area. You can also hire a coach. I think having a coach, or someone in that capacity, is a wonderful place to get support.

Keep in mind, people thrive on connection. When they're going through the divorce process, they often feel very alone. Maybe they feel ostracized by in-laws or any number of things, so I would say finding a group of people that are going through the same thing can be very empowering for them. At the same time, that can turn into a spiral of negativity if all anyone is doing is complaining about what's going on and complaining about their ex, this, that, and the other, but it's worthwhile to at least explore that option. Most professionals in an area should have some resources with regard to support systems for people going through divorce and separation.

Right, and you made a good point, too. You may have friends in happy marriages or you may have friends who are going through similar circumstances, and you don't want this engagement to devolve into a place of constant negativity. You want to surround yourself with people you can talk to that can relate to your experience, but are going to be a positive source of inspiration. I think that can be helpful.

It can give you that understanding that, "You know what? I'm not alone."

Exactly, and nobody wants to feel alone.

Closing Thoughts

You touched on it briefly, but as we conclude, can you summarize what outcomes you seek to help your clients achieve?

I want my clients to be able to disengage, to set boundaries, to recognize what they can and cannot control, and to be able to communicate as well as they can under the circumstances. I want them to be able to begin to recognize the things they can and cannot control and how that contributes to positive or negative communication.

You've made some great points, Maida, and offered some excellent advice. In conclusion, can you summarize some of the key pieces of advice you offer parents going through a divorce or going through a separation?

Absolutely. In tying everything together, I would advise individuals to set boundaries from the outset. I think this is the foundation for positive communication. It sets the tone for the process and, as I mentioned before, setting and maintaining healthy boundaries leads to freedom—but that freedom takes courage. One of the keys to a healthy divorce with kids is having healthy boundaries and more positive communication or, at least, more opportunity for positive communication.

To schedule a complimentary coaching session with Maida and discover the transformative impact of working with a Certified Divorce Coach, visit www.AlchemyCoaching.net. Sign up for her newsletter and get access to special deals on coaching packages and other services. To reach out to Maida directly, email her at mfarrar@gmail.com.

ABOUT MAIDA V. FARRAR, Esq., CDC

Maida Farrar is a Certified Divorce Coach who has spent a decade as a California Family Law Attorney. Having informally coached her clients for years while working as a divorce lawyer, Maida has found that her current role as Life Coach and Certified Divorce Coach allows her to pursue her passion for helping individuals navigate the divorce process, so that they get more of what they want with as little conflict as possible.

Maida helps her clients make informed decisions about the divorce process, set and maintain healthy boundaries, manage their emotions, set goals, create a workable action plan to achieve those goals, and find a balance between the legal process and moving on with their lives.

Maida specializes in working with single parents, helping them to feel in control, confident, and secure in their future so that they know their kids won't suffer. She offers a wide range of coaching services from individual coaching to group coaching to seminars and other events. She also and speaks to groups about the importance of setting boundaries, improved communication, and achieving optimal results while navigating divorce and separation.

Maida found that working with clients through the overwhelming process of divorce and separation eases much of the negative impact that divorce may have and allows her clients to move forward with confidence.

BUSINESS: Alchemy Coaching

WEBSITE: www.alchemycoaching.net

EMAIL: coach@alchemycoaching.net

PHONE: 916-930-6313

LOCATION: Vallejo, CA

FACEBOOK: www.facebook.com/thealchemycoach

TWITTER: www.twitter.com/alchemycoach1

LINKEDIN: www.linkedin.com/in/maida-farrar-99697710

INSTAGRAM: www.instagram.com/alchemycoaching

CHAPTER EIGHT

How to Help Your Teen Survive and Thrive After Divorce

by Nicola Beer

> *"Healthy families have nothing to do with whether the parents live together or apart. It is all to do with the love, support and life coping skills you provide your children with." — Nicola Beer*

Working with Nicola provided a myriad of breakthrough moments. She speaks with a candor and openness about her own personal experiences that makes her advice relatable and approachable to anyone who has gone through considerable pain and anguish, and what parent — who has gone through or going through divorce — hasn't experienced these emotions?

As a young teenager of 13, Nicola experienced firsthand the trauma and devastation that divorce can cause a teenager when parents unintentionally neglect the needs of their children. She witnessed her father move far away while her mother had a breakdown and became angry, even abusive. This left her feeling alone, anxious, angry and abandoned, while feeling compelled to balance her mother and father's needs. On the one hand, she didn't want to push her father further away. On the other hand, she didn't want to aggravate her mother and face the inevitable backlash. This balancing act caused her to bottle up her emotions—frustration, loneliness and pain that she carried into her twenties.

Through reflection and coaching, Nicola became aware that the support she craved for was also exactly what her mother needed during and after the divorce. Strategies to cope with the financial, logistical and emotional changes. Tips to deal with the stress, frustration, hurt and co-parenting challenges she was facing. Having managed to pull herself out of the pit of depression, she was able to release repressed anger, emotionally heal, and ultimately design and create her dream life. These experiences shaped who she is today, and inspired her to help others do the same.

Nicola is a relationship coach, therapist, podcaster, and author who is passionate about helping people achieve transformational results. She is certified in many different disciplines (Coaching, NLP, Hypnotherapy, Myer Briggs, Time Line Therapy®, Relationship Coaching, Addiction Recovery, Cellular, DNA Healing, The Journey®, Conflict Resolution and Family Therapy.)

Nicola is originally from England and now lives in beautiful Dubai, where she has built her practice—Pure Peace. In addition to working with clients in-person and across the world via Skype, she hosts clinics, trainings and retreats throughout the year in Dubai.

In our interview, Nicola shares her experiences and insights on several key topic areas important to parents raising teens during and after divorce:

- The most common challenges teens face and how parents can create an environment where they feel comfortable sharing their feelings and emotions.

- How can parents can overcome the challenge of knowing what to help their teenagers on, what their needs are, and when/how to do it.

- How to differentiate between typical teenage devel-opment issues and issues caused by divorce.

- The do's and don'ts of supporting teens through di-vorce.

- How and what to communicate with your teens about stressful situations.

- What the benefits are of working with a professional skilled across a variety of disciplines rather than relying solely on friends and family.

Jeremy: Nicola, it seems that most people who get into this field were inspired by their own life experiences, whether that was their own divorce or issues in their parents' divorce. I know you dealt with some traumatic issues as a teenager going through your own parent's divorce. Can you tell us a little bit about these experiences and how it has shaped your practice?

Nicola: Absolutely. My parents separated and got divorced when I was 13. My mother had a breakdown following the divorce and became very angry and abusive. Quite frankly, it was just a nightmare to live with. Dad, once the protector from my mother's anger, moved away. Instead of seeing him daily, it went from barely speaking to him or seeing him once every 6 or so weeks. It was a huge change.

I remember feeling angry, alone and depressed. But I had to hide these feelings because I feared if expressed them I might push my father even further away and I daren't show my mother, in case I aggravated her and have to face the repercussions, so I learned to repress them. In turn, this caused me to feel even more isolated. All I really wanted at the time was just someone to talk to, someone to help me through it, encourage me to focus on the future but there wasn't anyone there for me.

My turning point came when I was 14. I'm not proud of it, but I took 25 paracetamol feeling that I couldn't cope anymore and wanted to sleep and block it all out. My mother was forever shouting and stressed that she was bringing up 5 children with no money after the divorce. All I really wanted was just some peace. Peace in our home, peace between my parents, and the peace of mind that things will get better.

I ended up in the hospital, where my mother was watching me and told me not to say anything bad because she was concerned that they would take her away. I remember desperately wanting to share how I was feeling, but again, I had to swallow down that pain and suffering. The nurses, the doctors and my mom were all hostile towards me. It was there when I was lying in that hospital bed that I made a decision. The decision changed my life forever. The decision was that I deserved better and the realization that I would have to rely on myself to get out of this misery and create a better life. It just set me off onto this mission.

Over the next 10 years I studied psychology, mental health, sociology and did a lot of self-development work, which freed myself from this loneliness, this depression and an eating disorder. It allowed me to deal with the repressed anger. It was this long journey of self-healing. I decided that I needed to get myself both financially free, so that I could have the means to get out of the situation and emotionally free of the past. Even at 14, as soon as I left that hospital bed, I went and I got two part-time jobs. By the age of 15, I had 4,000 pounds in the bank. I was the first person in my family to go to university. I really drove myself into my studies and stayed motivated knowing I had to create a better future for myself.

I was proud of what I achieved by sheer determination, but it was the forgiveness part; the release of repressed anger I had against my parents that really made the difference. I realized it's not the money that gives you freedom — although that does help — but it's the emotional work that we do that provides true freedom.

At twenty-three years of age, I decided I wanted to help others do the same. I wanted to be there for people who have no one to talk to. I volunteered for an organization which is an emotional help line where anyone could call and just express any emotional distress, suicidal thoughts or other issues they were going through.

After doing that, I decided I really wanted to get into private coaching. I created a private coaching business. I helped people do the emotional healing work and create positive, lasting change.

Then, after a few years into doing that, I became familiar with divorce again because my sister went through it. Seeing how much my sister, her brother-in-law and her 4 children, who were age 4 to 16, were being affected. By affected, I mean panic attacks, depression, insomnia, aggression, blame, revenge, grief and loss. At that point, I decided that I would narrow my general life coaching to just focusing on marriage counseling, helping save marriages and then pre and post-divorce support.

Growing up having experienced these issues firsthand, I saw the need for parents and teenagers of divorce to have someone to talk to, someone to provide strategies to cope with the changes, because I firmly believe that divorce doesn't have to mean disaster. It can be an opportunity for growth, where closer bonds can be formed between parents and children, and a time where a new future can be created. That's why I set up Pure Peace to provide practical and emotional help to individuals, couples and families going through marriage breakdown and divorce.

It took me, Jeremy, years to heal and deal with the past. My mission is to share the tools I acquired so that others can get results in months and not years like it took me. Jeremy, I'm really certain that, had my mother had the support, had my siblings had the support, had I had the support, a divorce coach and someone to help us through, our childhood would have been radically different. This is what keeps me motivated to reach more people. That's why I love doing what I do and why I work with parents and teenagers to go from just surviving to really thriving after a divorce.

What sorts of emotions do you commonly see your clients dealing with and how do you help them?

Frustration, confusion, hurt and despair are all common emotions following a divorce for both adults and children. I focus on helping parents deal with the emotional roller coaster and stress that divorce brings so that they feel stronger and better equipped to support themselves and their children through it.

The problem that many parents struggle with is how best to help their children. Many unintentionally say or do the wrong thing, especially when it comes to teenagers. Often, parents will come to me concerned about their teenager's grades, angry outbursts, withdrawal, sadness or refusal to see one parent. This can be pre-divorce, during divorce or after divorce.

I guide them on how to minimize the long term impact di-vorce has on children by educating them on grief and loss, and providing them with a series of actions they can take to move themselves and their children forward.

Often, I get asked by parents to work with teenagers directly. That involves providing out a confidential safe place for teenagers to open up about their feelings around divorce where together we work towards common goals that they really want to achieve and also managing the difficult feelings that sometimes divorce can bring.

Lastly, as co-parenting can be a major challenge in and of itself, I provide tools and strategies to reduce hostility, increase collaboration and peace in the co-parenting relationship. A lot of people will come to me and say, "But my ex is extremely difficult," or, "My teenager is a nightmare." Even if you feel that it won't work for you, there are often strategies we can do to lessen the conflict. That's actually why I call the business Pure Peace, because whether it's peace of mind the individuals are seeking or peace between husband and wife, teenagers and parents or between ex's co-parenting, the programs I employ are specifically designed to restore and build peace. That's why I called it Pure Peace.

Challenges Teens Face During Divorce

Nicola, no doubt, divorce is challenging for everybody. What are some of the most common challenges that teenagers have when it comes to knowing how to help them through this difficult process?

When it comes to teenagers and divorce, many parents be-come confused over what to do and what not to do. They wonder if teenagers should be left alone altogether, to deal with the divorce or whether they need to focus and talk to them and spend time with them. It can be quite a challenge to know the difference between typical teenager issues versus something that's being caused by the separation of the divorce.

Common concerns parents have are how to deal with poor school performance, angry outbursts, hostility, sadness and a lack of interest in family life. Claire [not her real name], for example, is a lady I work with to help resolve concerns around her teenagers. Claire had physical custody of her teenage children — age 14 to 16 — until about 6 months ago. Then, she gave physical custody to her ex-husband so that the teenagers wouldn't have to leave their schools, friends and sports clubs. She moved an hour away and lived in a new four-bedroom house. She went to great lengths to ensure that they had her own rooms exactly how they wanted them. Claire agreed that she would see them Tuesday night and every weekend. She'd been keeping in contact, seeing the short space in between those times, but she felt totally crushed because they decided they didn't want to come and stay anymore. She said to me, "Nicola, you know, I feel like giving up. They're moving further and further away. Should I make them see me or shall I just give up? You know, I'm sure my ex is bad mouthing me. I don't know what to do. I'm tired, I'm hurt and I'm frustrated. Help me know what to do."

This is exactly the challenge that a lot of parents have when it comes to teenagers of divorce. It's whether to leave the teenagers be and accept, "Oh, I don't want to see you," or whether to take action and intervene. That is what I'd say is the biggest challenge when it comes to teenagers.

Raising a teenager is definitely a challenge - whether you're married or not. But in the context of divorce, like Claire's situation, it is even more difficult. How can parents better understand what their teenagers' needs are how to support them?

They need to understand 3 things. First, to be sensitive to the typical teenager development process. Second parents need to understand about the losses divorce brings and how to support teenagers through the loss. And, also they need to look out for the three most common warning signs that indicate your teenager probably needs intervention.

After sharing these with Claire, for example, she felt much more confident in what action to take and how to speak to her teenagers in a non-confrontational way.

Supporting Teens Through Transition

You say parents of teenagers need to educate themselves on a number of different things. Can you expound on each of these?

Be sensitive to the typical teenager development process.

Typical teenage development: In order to help you and your teenagers through divorce, it's important to acknowledge what is typical in teenage development and what isn't. I've had the privilege of supporting many parents through divorce and often when their teenager wants to spend less time with them or is testing their boundaries, they automatically think that it must be the ex badmouthing them, but accusing your ex of badmouthing you and blaming them rather than accepting your teenager for being a typical teenager can cause irreversible damage to your co-parenting relationship. What children of all ages need most is for their parents to at least be civil, because the higher the conflict, the more stress and destruction divorce can bring for everyone involved.

Typical teenage development insights: Teenagers want independence. As teenagers grow, so does their desire to be independent. They want to make their own decisions but they still need their parent's support. They're likely to want to spend time in the house where they have the greatest freedom. Teenagers also test boundaries. Though it may seem that they're rebelling against you and what you stand for, they are attempting to identify what is important to them. Thirteen to 18 is a time where we work on solidifying our identity and establishing our sense of self and who we are, in relation to the rules and regulations of society. It's where we reject and accept different viewpoints. This means your teenagers may push you to the limits on your rules or to test you to see if you will continue to enforce the rules and stick by your values.

Teenagers also have a desire to be with friends. Through teenage friendships, teens discover who they are, what they want and where they belong in the community, what music, subjects, sports and activities they keep or get into. It's important to understand and encourage them to be with their friends and as parents, not to take it personally or think that again, it's the ex doing the badmouthing. Teenagers also may develop a crush on someone and be very preoccupied, thinking about this and want alone time.

In general, teenagers want less from their parents. Divorced parents I work with find it difficult when they realize that their teenager doesn't need them as much anymore. Compared to younger children, teenagers want less of their parent's time, less of their advice, opinions and less of the togetherness. What many parents I coach forget or don't see is that this is often typical teenager behavior and not necessarily a result of the divorce or of the ex being difficult.

How to support teenagers through loss.

Helping teenagers through loss and understanding the loss: This is another really important component. When helping teenagers deal with divorce, the key is to understand the losses they face and help them deal with those losses. Divorce to a teenager can bring about many losses at once. There's a loss of seeing the parents as frequently. There's a loss of expectation, that the family will be together. Realizing that perhaps birthdays and Christmases will never be the same again. There's a loss of childhood. There's a loss of trust, a loss of faith in relationships, marriage and love, loss of school, loss of familiarity and routines, loss of residence or change of residence.

Acknowledge and accept their feelings: Acknowledge that they may feel sad, they may feel disappointed, angry, frustrated and/or anxious about the future. They may also miss the other parent. One of the most important things you can do is to allow your teenager to express how they feel and welcome it and accept it without trying to fix it or fix them. That's where most parents fall into the trap of trying to fix their children's emotions during divorce. Feelings are just feelings and need to be accepted as such.

Don't try to "fix" them. What do I mean by fixing? Let me just give you a few examples of what not to say to teenagers when they express how they feel. If a teenager, for example, says that they feel sad, they feel bad, they feel upset.

One of the worst things you can say to them is not to feel sad because no one should ever be told not to feel how they feel. That's confusing because it's impossible to do. Think about it, how can you not feel? Instead, you can help them by saying things like, "Yes, I sometimes feel sad about the divorce and the changes. When I feel sad, I call a friend. Would you like to have a friend come over?" Listening and accepting allows them to feel safe in expressing how they feel which is key in healthy recovery after divorce. You're also giving them a coping mechanism, if you're suggesting a way they can cope with them.

> *"Listening and accepting allows [teenagers] to feel safe in expressing how they feel which is key in healthy recovery after divorce."*

Don't tell your teen, "Just be strong." Another unhelpful thing to say to your teenager is, "be strong." Many teenagers and parents going through or coming out of divorce have shared with me that they've been told by others to be strong. This is bad advice because it is also impossible to do. If you think about it, you can either be strong or you can be human. Being strong implies hiding and repressing your emotions which is not good for the mind or the body. In order to deal with a divorce, you need to feel what you feel. Personally, I remember being told to be strong from my younger brother and my sisters in the divorce, which was really unsettling and unfair. I felt as if I wasn't allowed to react to the divorce and that my feelings weren't accepted. This is really common among teenagers, if they have younger siblings they're often told, "Put a brave face on" or "Let's keep it together for your younger brother or sister". Sometimes, that can be really difficult for them. I know I keep repeating myself but it's really important to accept whatever feelings your teenagers have.

Don't try to fix feelings with sugar, junk food or other gifts. Thirdly, another mistake that I see lots of people make is using food or gifts to fix feelings. I was guilty of this myself before I became aware of it and learned a healthier way to deal with grief and loss. What do I mean? Imagine this scenario of a 13-year-old girl who is crying because she misses one parent, in an attempt to "cheer her up" I've heard parents, saying "Don't feel sad. Let's get some ice cream, or order a take out tonight" Or for a teenage boy who is angry, gets taken to buy some new football boots. This is where caring and loving parents mistakenly try to fix feelings with sugar, junk food or items. We often learn this from when we are 2 or 3 years old and get sweets if we fall over and hurt ourselves in the playground. But these fixes don't help us process the changes. They may serve as a temporary distraction away from our feelings but it does nothing to help us deal with them long-term and recover. Anything that distracts us can take away from allowing the normal, natural grief and loss process to happen.

If we're not given other strategies to deal with loss, as adults, we may develop emotional habits like: comfort eating, drinking, smoking, chocolating, shopping, gambling in an attempt to avoid our feelings and thoughts. This is not to blame parents for giving treats to their children. Absolutely not. This is about being aware that when it comes to sharing feelings, we need to first listen and allow them to express themselves without trying to fix them.

Look out for the three most common warning signs.

I mentioned also that are 3 warning signs to look out for. The 3 warning signs you need to look out for are:

1. Turning inward: depression, extreme sadness, isola-tion, withdrawal, guilt or self-blame and a change in eating patterns

2. Turning outward: aggression, angry outbursts, bully-ing others, rebelling, refusal to participate in school or other activities

3. Guilt. Feeling Guilty: blaming themselves for the di-vorce or feeling torn and bad when spending time with the other parent.

Often teenagers can turn inwards during a divorce. Separation from parents is normal but if a teen completely withdraws from parents, from activities, from friends, then they may need additional attention and support.

I was working with a sixteen-year-old teenage girl. She said that the reason she stopped seeing her friends is because she felt like she brought negative energy with her everywhere she went and that the divorce and her new step-family made her feel abandoned. She couldn't help but think that her life had been ruined, ruined forever. She just went around thinking, "My life has been ruined." Because of that, she didn't want to be the girl at school with the problems. She didn't want to burden her friends. So she'd convinced herself that they and she were better off alone. She said that she lost her appetite completely and was just feeling extremely lonely. The lonelier and angrier she felt, the more she just isolated herself from other people. What she really needed was someone she could talk to who wouldn't judge her for the anger and sadness she felt; someone who could help her come up with coping strategies.

If your teenager is going inwards or displaying prolonged sadness, encourage them to talk with someone they trust, perhaps a family friend, an uncle or an aunt, or an expert coach. And, encourage them to spend time with friends and be more sociable because isolation can feed more isolation. That's when they can become more withdrawn. It's really important to notice if your child is turning inward.

Then, there are teenagers who turn outward. Sometimes, a teenager will turn their frustrations outward through aggres-sive behavior, rebelling or angry outbursts. Usually when a teenager's acting out, they want to either teach their parents a lesson or to punish them. They're acting out to communicate how angry and upset they are. They need acknowledgement and understanding to move past this.

I work with many teenagers. I find that often all they need if they are turning outwards are tools to express their anger and emotions in a much healthier way. Too often, they lack the knowledge on how to release anger so they just hold it in and then they just erupt.

In my work, I'll take parents and teenagers through tools to educate them that anger is a natural and normal human emotion. It's not bad in itself. It's not a problem to feel angry, but it's the way that it's expressed that causes a problem. It's about giving them a choice on how they channel their anger. For some, that can be playing sports, running, martial arts, art therapy, talking. It's also about helping identify where it's coming from so that we can then tackle any deeper issues.

> *"...anger is a natural and normal human emotion. It's not bad in itself. It's not a problem to feel angry, but it's the way that it's expressed that causes a problem. It's about giving them a choice on how they channel their anger."*

Lastly then, there's guilt. It's important to reinforce children of all ages that the divorce is not their fault. They are not to blame. Even if the parents are arguing during the divorce, or after the divorce, it's not their fault. That's what they really do need: reassurance. Also, teenagers can feel guilty about leaving one parent because the parent really needs them. They feel guilty about whether the parent they have left will be alone, unhappy and sad. Here, parents really need to encourage teenagers to have a relationship with both parents.

Nicola, you bring up some really interesting points because often times, the relationship between parents broke down because of that feeling of lack of comfort to express oneself and bottling up those feelings. A lot of what you've brought up is managing emotions, being comfortable with one's emotions and being able to share that in a comforta-ble

environment with their parents. I think what you're saying is that parents, they shouldn't pass blame or judgment. They should make their children feel comfortable that they can express themselves in constructive and positive ways rather than turning to destructive behaviors. Is that correct?

Yes, absolutely. These are the warning signs. These are the signs where if it becomes extreme, then additional support could be of great benefit.

You used your client, Claire, as an example. I'm just curious about her situation and her teenage children. How did things work out for Claire?

With Claire, we discussed her teenager's behavior and decided that the best action would be for her and her husband to speak to the teenagers together. Despite barely speaking to each other, Claire and her husband, Ian [not his real name], had a call separately with me first and then Ian agreed that, yes, it would be good to speak to them. The sixteen-year-old son Luke didn't actually want to stay with Claire because he was interested in a girl at a skate park and that the skate park was next to his father's house. Claire then made the weekends more acceptable to Luke by saying that he could do both. "On the weekends, you stay with me. I'll take you to the skate park." That problem was solved very quickly. Many problems have easier solutions than we may expect.

Kate, their daughter, was still struggling. She didn't say much when they sat down and spoke to her. They offered her the opportunity to speak with me, to see if she would open up more then. When I spoke with Kate, she shared that she didn't want to stay with her mum because she felt that she was abandoning her dad and she felt sorry for her dad; she blamed her mother for the divorce which made her not want to stay with her anymore. When her brother voiced he didn't want to go, she believed he felt the same as her, that it was the mother's fault for the divorce and that she shouldn't leave her dad either.

Talking it through with her, we built some trust. I often go first with teenagers and explain how I felt so they feel com-fortable.

Kate said to me that I could have permission to share this with her parents so that the issue and her feelings could be accepted and resolved. Her parents took this on board. They then sat down together and explained that the divorce wasn't just Claire's fault. For the first time, they explained the differences that they had (without the details) so the daughter could accept what had happened. They encouraged her and said to her that she needed to love both of them, that she didn't have to pick sides. This really helped her. Also, her dad, Ian, promised that he would focus on having some of his own hobbies and doing more in his own life so that his daughter wouldn't have to worry about him being home alone when she wasn't there. As parents, you need to reassure your children that they don't need to choose sides and encourage them to have a relationship with both of you.

Through talking, they managed to resolve the issues. Now, they both stay with Claire every other weekend too, which is what Claire wanted and what's best for the teenagers.

The Do's and Don'ts of Supporting Teens Through Divorce

That's great to hear that they were able to work it out by simply communicating and agreeing to solve the issue collaboratively. What are some other things parents can do to support teenagers through a divorce?

There is a lot that parents can do, and I'll go through each:

Do keep as much routine as possible.

One of the things they can do is keep as much routine as possible because whether teenagers will admit it or not, they like routine and they like familiarity. Familiarity brings safety. When helping a teenager through divorce, it's important to limit the amount of additional changes wherever that's possible, as well as try to stick to similar rules at both homes. Rules around seeing friends, homework, bedtime, a united co-parenting front can really go a long way.

"...stick to similar rules at both homes. Rules around seeing friends, homework, bedtime, a united co-parenting front can really go a long way."

Do allow and encourage them to have a childhood.

Another thing which is really important is to be conscious of is ensuring that teenagers don't lose their childhood. Allow and encourage them to be teenagers, to play "muck about" etc. Feeling a loss of childhood is common among teenage children where they try to support the parents by taking over extra household responsibilities. If they have younger siblings in particular, they can often feel responsible for helping them through the divorce. They may be concerned about whether they need to contribute financially. If teenagers are left to take on too many extra responsibilities, too much emotional burden, they can stop fantasizing about their own future and family and instead worry about their parents' emotional distress. You really have to make sure you're allowing your teenager to still have a childhood.

"...stick to similar rules at both homes. Rules around seeing friends, homework, bedtime, a united co-parenting front can really go a long way."

Do allow and encourage them to have a childhood.

Another thing which is really important is to be conscious of is ensuring that teenagers don't lose their childhood. Allow and encourage them to be teenagers, to play "muck about" etc. Feeling a loss of childhood is common among teenage children where they try to support the parents by taking over extra household responsibilities. If they have younger siblings in particular, they can often feel responsible for helping them through the divorce. They may be concerned about whether they need to contribute financially. If teenagers are left to take on too many extra responsibilities, too much emotional burden, they can stop fantasizing about their own future and family and instead worry about their parents' emotional distress. You really have to make sure you're allowing your teenager to still have a childhood.

> *"If teenagers are left to take on too many extra responsibilities, too much emotional burden, they can stop fantasizing about their own future and family and instead worry about their parents' emotional distress. You really have to make sure you're allowing your teenager to still have a childhood."*

Do help them understand the divorce without sharing unnecessary details.

Another thing which is really important when it comes to teenagers and divorce is to help them understand the divorce. It's important that teenagers are kept out of adult problems. When it comes to the details of divorce, infidelity, sexual incompatibility, these should never be shared. However, teenagers do benefit from being told about the good and the not so good points in marriage. If they're given reasons without the details, it enables them to draw life lessons from the experience of divorce, not to dwell on it and not to dwell on wondering what went wrong. A teenager can be terrified that they may repeat their parents' mistakes in love, in marriage, in romance. Many question if they're capable of sustaining relationships themselves.

If they are given some kind of picture of what happens, it can help to calm the anxiety. The picture could be along the lines of something simple like, "We fell out of love, our interests changed, we grew apart, we wanted different futures, we couldn't agree on certain things," but it's always better to say something than nothing when it comes to teenagers.

Teenagers are also more likely than younger children to form their own opinion of why the marriage ended. Many teenagers think that the parents should never have got married. They may criticize one or both of their parents. If they express this opinion, just allow them to have it. Don't get angry or defensive. Advise them that things can just seem very different from the outside than inside the relationship and that you're glad that they felt comfortable enough to express their point of view.

Do be careful when it comes to dating again.

Another thing which is really important on the "do list" when it comes to teenagers is, do be careful around dating again. Teenagers are much more likely to worry about their parents' dating and stepfamilies than younger children are. They may feel threatened or worry for the other parent, having to do with the other parent's new partner. They also may worry about how the siblings are going to be treated. I've worked with teenagers who've spent so much emotional energy thinking about their mother's or father's new partners that they've let it consume them. This is not healthy for teenager to be so concerned with parents' lovers.

What do you do? The best way, again, is to calm this anxiety; talk to them about their feelings around your dating or your ex's dating. These conversations should be handled delicately and be solution focused; so look at how they're feeling and what solutions you can provide or how you can make them feel more comfortable.

Do support their academic pursuits.

Another really, really, really important area and this is actually why many parents come to me is around school, exams, college and homework. It's important that through the divorce, you give extra support in these areas. Often, changes in home can disrupt school performance. Consistency, when it comes to homework, parents evening, and school activities is important. Some teenagers can lose focus. Helping them refocus is critical. In fact, one of the topics I work with teenagers and young adults in most is to help them get good grades at school and college after divorce. The key here is motivation. Teenagers need to see and set goals for themselves and to think about their own future and not about the divorce.

Often when I work with teenagers, I take them through a Myers-Briggs personality assessment tool which is an online personality type report. Teenagers then feel great, that they can understand more about themselves, their personality, their interest, their career options. This can be a very beneficial way when they're going through the divorce to refocus on themselves and build greater momentum and excitement for their future.

When we're talking about grades, sometimes teenagers' grades can slip because they don't know how to cope with the changes that divorce brings, the losses divorce brings, from staying in different homes and changing school grades. You want to support them through this and ask them if they need any help.

Other times, there are occasions where I've spoken to teenagers and the reason they are allowing their grades to slip is because they want to punish their parents or get attention from them. If this is the case it's about helping teenagers to see that this is going to harm them and getting the parents to give them that attention, to understand and help them through the pain and the suffering that they're going through. It's about helping them take responsibility for their grades, and create a plan for their future. It's really important throughout all of this to explain to teenagers that yes change can be difficult, it can be uncomfortable and unsettling at first, but it can also be an opportunity to grow and create new exciting opportunities. I think they really need that reassurance.

You spoke about the things parents should be doing. Can you share with us what parents should not do with teenagers?

Don'ts are just as important as the do's when it comes to teenagers experiencing their parents' divorce:

Don't share your adult problems with your teenagers.

The first is, don't share your adult problems with your teenagers. Share adult problems with adults. Teenage children do not need to know the reason for marriage breakdown, affairs that took place, financial disputes, breakdowns caused by lack of affection, sex, or love. These never need to be divulged. I've spoken to teenagers where they've been told by their parents the other parent sleeps around or they have rejected them or they gambled money or they're an addict. This can be too much for teenagers to process.

As mentioned at the beginning, feelings of frustration, confusion, hurt and despair are all common emotions following a divorce, but seeking solace by confiding in teenagers is not good for them. Teenagers are just not prepared or equipped to deal with the parents' emotional load during and after the divorce, because they're so overwhelmed dealing with their own emotions, their own changes and their own losses they're going through.

I've worked with some teenagers who felt so responsible for their parents' emotional well-being that they don't want to leave their side, where parents have shared how sad they are and how depressed they are. The teenager will then want to sit next to them every night, to be there for them. This is just not healthy. Teenagers need freedom to be with their friends, away from their parents.

My tip here is to get support. It's definitely important for you to deal with your own concerns, disappointment and stress during this time and find someone that you can talk to who will give you coping strategies, someone that will listen and help you move forward, because the stronger and healthier you are, the better off your children will be.

Don't have financial conflicts in front of your teenagers or ignore financial changes altogether.

Teenagers do not need to know who is paying more or less for their upbringing. This is an adult conversation and should stay that way. When teenagers hear their parents argue over their expenses, they start to blame themselves for causing the problems. Many teenagers have said to me that they feel unwanted, like a burden. As you can imagine, this is extremely painful for them to feel. Don't ask them to get money off the other parent either, because that just adds more awkwardness and stress to their lives.

> *"When teenagers hear their parents argue over their expenses, they start to blame themselves for causing the problems."*

When it comes to finances, don't ignore financial changes altogether with teenagers, because when it comes to finances, keep in mind that teenagers are more aware of what things cost and changes that happen during divorce. They may worry about being poor. They may worry about affording necessary items, school trips and college. Adjusting these concerns is important, and you may do well to assure them they will have enough money for essentials. But, they may have less money for non-essentials like holidays or certain activities. Also, explain, if you are downsizing houses, that it doesn't mean they're poor. They're still going to have enough money for essentials but as a family, you're just being careful.

My advice here is to discuss finances with your ex in private and hire a co-parenting coach if you're really struggling with agreeing on the finances. If they happen to hear you fight, reassure them your financial disputes are not their fault. They're not to blame for any changes in financial circumstances.

Don't badmouth your ex.

Another major don't here and I've mentioned this a few times through our conversation together, Jeremy. And, that's, don't badmouth your ex. We may hear this, but many parents may not realize what badmouthing the ex means or what consequences and damage it can have. It may seem obvious not to badmouth the ex, but many parents engage in it anyway. However, it's extremely important that you never badmouth your ex; they will always be the father or mother of your children.

> *"Teenagers develop better when they're free to love and respect each parent based on their own experience of them."*

Many parents, during and after a divorce, experience waves of anger, hurt and resentment and can benefit immensely from sharing frustrations with someone but this someone should never be the teenager as I mentioned. It can be so hard not to explode when your ex break promises and lets you down, or even worse, if they let your children down. It may take a lot of restraint to hold back from badmouthing them, but it's so important for your teenager because teenagers are already processing and dealing with their own feelings around the divorce that you do hold back. They're often confused about what's happening and what they're feeling. They don't need the added confusion of their parents' negative views and opinions about each other.

Teenagers develop better when they're free to love and respect each parent based on their own experience of them. They should be able to make their own judgments. My mother repeatedly told me, "Your dad doesn't love you, because he's not paying anything for you," and, "Your dad doesn't care about you because he's not giving us any money." As a teenager, I thought that that was true. I believed my mum. I thought my dad didn't love or care for us anymore but it wasn't true at all. My dad left the house to my mum and had to start over with nothing. He was unable to give much during the first few years of the divorce as he was struggling to start over again himself. But he did pay all the child support for 5 children. I didn't know this until many years later.

This badmouthing had huge consequences for me. I believed that when someone spends money on you, they love you. If they don't spend any money on you, that means that they don't love you or they don't care for you. What a disaster this belief played out when I was dating throughout my whole 20s. Men who bought me gifts, took me to nice places, regardless of how they treated me, I thought they loved me. Caring fellows who didn't have much money and were really caring and did sweet things for me, I thought, "Well, they don't really care about me because they're not buying me things. I must be not good enough. They're not caring for me. They don't love me." Thankfully, through coaching and all the self-development work I mentioned, I let these twisted beliefs go.

This is just a minor example of the consequences badmouthing can have. If it gets really extreme, many teenagers lose contact with their parents forever and they can miss out on a lifetime of love and support from a parent. That is really, really where badmouthing can have devastating consequences, because, yes, it may hurt the other parent if they don't have a relationship with their teenager, but it hurts the teenager just as much.

It's important to remember, and I touched on this earlier, that teenagers of divorce will form ideas around love, trust, relationships and marriage from their parents, from the divorce and from those years. If they're being told by their parents that the other parent did this or did that, they're going to base their love and their marriage values and relationship values around their parents' negative experiences. I had one teenager who said she doesn't think she can trust a man because her mamma told her that all men cheat. That was affecting her in her adolescence because she had grown to believe that all men will cheat on her. Her jealously and insecurities often got out of control. Whenever we go through significant painful emotional events, it's normal to create distorted beliefs. That's why it's so important that parents really do watch everything that they say.

Don't use your teenager as a messenger.

Teenagers should not be responsible for giving messages to the other parent, especially for delivering unhappy news. Many teenagers I've spoken to get really stressed when they have to relay messages that the other parent doesn't want to. It could be about vacations, finances, or school activities. Typically, the teenager will have to deliver messages that the parent doesn't want to do, because they think that it's going to get an angry reaction. It's unfair to put onto the teenager to deliver bad news when they're going to face anger from one of the other parents. It's also going to affect the time that they have together with that parent. It puts them in an awkward position. They may not even share whatever you wanted them to share. That can create more hostility in the co-parenting relationship if you're thinking that a message is going to be relayed and the message isn't relayed.

Teenagers are also often asked to report back on how the other parent is doing, basically spying, to find out whether they've got a new relationship or how they're spending their finances. Such requests, again, put an unnecessary moral dilemma on teenagers because if they don't report back, they feel that, "I'm not pleasing mum because she's asked me for information on dad and I don't want to tell her." But, if they do give into mum and they do say, "Yes, he's got a new girlfriend," or, "Yes, he's doing this or he's doing that," then they feel like they're betraying their dad because their dad shared and trusted the new information with them. Any request of information is putting them into an awkward, no-win situation, as teenagers know spying and gossiping is wrong.

I had an eighteen-year-old share with me how her parent's divorce had been so hard for them, not because of any of the other losses or changes, but particularly around the spying on whether they're dating again, whether their new partner is attractive, whether they're a nice person, whether they've bought anything for them, whether they've treated them to anything. The obsession by both their parents to know who their other partner is, what money they're spending or splashing around, made the teenager not even want to see either of them.

Think before you ask. Do you really need to know more information about your ex? If yes and you have personal questions, ask your ex directly when the children are not present and just accept their answers as true. Some parents can't even talk with the other parent, and I can understand that, but fortunately we've got modern technology. We can email or text. Or even use a coach or meditator.

Don't use your teenager as a weapon.

And, finally, the last thing I want to talk about that I think is really important is, don't use teenagers as a weapon. The intense feeling of anger and hurt can often result in a desire to get revenge or to teach a spouse a lesson. I hear parents come to me, and say, "You know, I really want to get him back for the way he treated me. I really want him to feel the pain that I am feeling." It can be very tempting for parents to act on such impulses and aim to manipulate or restrict access to children as a way of punishment or to blame them for the teenager's problems. You may not think the ex deserves to spend time with your teenagers. You may feel that, especially if they've caused a divorce and not paying what they should and not treating you properly or them properly, that you're going to restrict access. **But denying your teenager a relationship with a parent hurts them just as much as it does the parent.**

> *"It begs the question, but I feel this question is really important: do you love your teenager more than you detest your ex?"*

Obviously, if there's a genuine concern for their safety, this is a different story. It should be handled appropriately, but restricting access is not the only way.

Jeremy, too often I see parents using children as a weapon against the other parent. Restricting the other parent's access to the children can be emotionally traumatic and damaging to kids of all ages. Beyond restricting access, I also see parents using teenagers as a weapon by blaming the other parent for any of the teenager's changes or problems.

Teenagers may have depression, eating disorders, anger, issues with school grades, failure in school, and it may be tempting to fault these issues on the other parent. Few other things are more hurtful than for a teenager to witness than their behavior, emotional issue or problem being used as a weapon in a fight against the other parent.

Personally, I know this because I've been there. When my parents got a divorce and broke down, my mum became very difficult and my dad moved away. I had a lot of repressed anger at my mum and at my dad. I felt alone, frustrated and very angry. I couldn't control the situation at home. I couldn't control my mother's anger. I couldn't control the fact that my dad had moved away. I couldn't control that there was never any peace. Unfortunately, I went on to control the only thing I could... my food. I began to restrict my food and very quickly, became very, very thin. My mother used it to blame my father for it. My father said, "Well, you know, she's living with you. It's not my fault." I felt ten times worse because they weren't talking to me about my eating. Instead, they were using and spending all of their emotional energy on blaming each other. I couldn't believe I was being used in this way, I needed help, not to be a weapon in their war.

This case is not unusual. I see this time and time again. Many teenagers who aren't getting the grades they once did, they're having trouble at school or any other changes which could just be, again, part of the normal teenage development I mentioned, they are being used as a weapon to hurt the other one. They may say, "You're doing this to our teenager. You're doing that." Parents really need to question whether blaming the other parent will help their children. Often what is needed is a collaborative, co-parenting effort to support teenagers through any issues. If your teenager is going through changes and you are concerned, you need to work with your teenager, with your ex and possibly with the school as a team, rather than being aggressive towards each other.

Predictable in divorce, finances are always stressful. It's always an issue, and teenagers tend to have a lot of expenses. You spoke eloquently about the consequences of badmouthing one's ex and blaming them for not having enough money to do things. How in your own situation, you grew up equating a romantic interest spending money on you with love. And, when you met someone who was kind but did not have much money, must not love you.

What is the best way for a parent to communicate with their child or children, or to their teenagers, in those situations where finances are stressful and they are tempted to shift blame? How do they best communicate that it's not anybody's fault in particular – that this is just the reality of the situation?

That's a really good question. I think the way to do it, is just explain to them that divorce is a change. With divorces, there are changes in finances. We may have less for the short term, or we may have less and we may have to downsize. We're just being careful. When you go from one house to 2 houses, there are going to be some cutbacks. Explain to them that "we may have to budget, but there will be enough for your essentials. For non-essential items, we'll talk about it and we'll work out what we can afford and what we can't afford. We understand, as a teenager, you're going to have growing needs. When you need something, let's sit down and we'll see if we can reach an agreement to help you with that."

Then, the parents need to be flexible and have open dialog between each other saying, "This has come up. There's a skiing trip. Shall we say, 'No' to this trip or shall we work together?", or "Do you have the money at the moment? I don't have the money." It's about taking each case as it comes but teenagers definitely need to know that they're going to have enough for their essentials. I think that's really important.

Knowing When to Enlist Outside Support

Clearly, there are a lot of things for parents to consider and to learn. What would you say is the most important thing for parents to consider?

I think the most important thing to consider is when to get some outside support. Many individuals and parents going through divorce procrastinate when it comes to getting some support or leaving it until it's too late. Just like in marriage counseling, couples come to me when the relationship is almost completely destroyed. Parents can do the same. Sometimes, by then, the damage is really great, when it didn't need to get so bad.

At the beginning, many parents wonder whether they need any guidance or whether they can resolve things on their own. Of course, it may be possible to tackle issues without any support at all, but many have shared with me that before working together, they were more stressed, there was more drama and chaos in their lives. There was more conflict in their co-parenting relationship

As I mentioned, it took me years to feel like my old self again. No one should have to wait years. It breaks my heart where I see individuals suffer. They come to me and they've been waiting 5 to 10, even 30 years to feel better after a divorce. Children only grow up once; they're only teenagers for a short time. So I believe every effort should be made to help the parents and the teenagers enjoy it.

> *"Children only grow up once; they're only teenagers for a short time. So I believe every effort should be made to help the parents and the teenagers enjoy it."*

I think that's the greatest thing. I appreciate that many people reading this may be thinking, "Well, I'm not sure if it'll work for me. Nicola, you don't know my teenagers or my ex," which is a valid point because I don't know that. It can be hard to see if anything will work if they're a nightmare to deal with right now. In truth, the only way to find out is to get in touch with an expert and have a session with them, try it.

I offer a complementary new beginning session and that takes away the risk for parents. To qualify to have this session with me, you must really want to change things and move forward. In this session, we'll cover where you are now, where your children are now and where you want to be. Where's the gap? We'll list any hidden challenges in your way of reaching where you want to be. Then, we'll define a list of action steps that you can take to move forward. There's no obligation. It's just an opportunity to explore for those who, again, really want to change things and move forward. This can be booked through my website.

When it comes to hiring an expert, a lot of parents reflexively think they just need to hire an attorney. Most attorneys have not been trained or educated in psychology or sociology or therapy or anything like that – nor should they be a therapist. Why is it so beneficial and imperative that parents hire somebody such as yourself who's been trained across a variety of disciplines?

I think experts understand what you're going through because they've helped hundreds of people through the same. They should have programs and packages that will help you to get the results you're after, where you can track your progress and move forward. Without experts, coming out of a divorce, you may needlessly suffer longer and struggle with more stress and drama.

Many come to me wondering if they'll always be single, if they'll ever meet someone new, if they'll be able to love and trust a new partner. They wonder if they'll be able to survive financially and if they can raise their teenagers to be healthy and successful. Yes, this is all possible. This can all be achieved with the right mindset and sequence of steps, but if you don't have any support and you lack the framework to help you reach those goals, it can be very difficult.

While there's benefit in expressing your feelings to friends, family members and colleagues, they can also give conflicting or biased advice. This can leave you with more confusion and uncertainty than before you opened up. It's important to be careful and cautious in the advice you take from others.

The other danger in opening up to non-experts is that you can sometimes be made to feel worse, often unintentionally, but this can cause you to isolate further or fake recovery. I've seen this happen a lot, people faking recovery, pretending that everything is fine. It can be physically and mentally exhausting, to put on an act and pretend everything is great. It also diverts our attention away from the real issues that need to be addressed. This often slows down or prevents the normal recovery process.

Another big issue I come across is that when we're going through difficult times or facing a particular problem, we subconsciously seek out people who will validate what we want to hear, rather than what we need to hear. We're all guilty of this; I'm guilty of it myself. Often we call people we know who will make us feel better by agreeing with whatever we're saying, but in order to move forward through a divorce, you need to have someone who is not only encouraging, but also constructive and honest. You need someone who is equipped with the knowledge and tools to hold you accountable to implement the agreed-upon plans. Friends may just say, "You know, don't worry," or, "Just be yourself." But, they're not trained, nor are they experts. An expert may put demands on you, but they will encourage you to move forward in the right direction.

This is why, personally, I've hired experts throughout my life to help me create change. I've found experts who are really effective; I've worked with cooking instructors, nutritionists, personal trainers, business and marketing coaches, career coaches throughout my lifetime, because they help you create that change when you feel that you need that in your life.

Closing Thoughts

Are there any other final words of advice you have before we conclude?

I just want to say one thing. Divorce is always a difficult transition. The way that parents handle it can greatly influence how well teenagers cope. For parents reading this, you really can make a difference as to how divorce happens. Divorce does not need to be a disaster. You do have the power to influence and support their teenagers through it.

Nicola offers a free report on her website— "Protect Your Children through Divorce and Avoid the 3 Most Common Mistakes". You can download this for free at www.purepeacecoaching.com/protectchildren.

You can also listen to her podcast show for free "Divorce Talk with Nicola Beer" where Nicola covers topics such as how to deal with anger, what to do if your ex badmouths you, what to do if your teenager doesn't want to see you, and the importance of establishing joint rules when co-parenting. Her podcast is available at www.purepeacecoaching.com/listen or through iTunes and Stitcher Radio—search "Divorce Talk with Nicola Beer."

If you would like to book a complimentary "new beginning consultation" or get additional support, you may contact Nicola through the Pure Peace Coaching website. She interfaces with people in person and through Skype sessions across the globe.

ABOUT NICOLA BEER

Nicola Beer is an international relationship & divorce coach and best-selling author. She helps individuals in-person and online via skype to emotionally heal and create a new beginning.

Nicola felt alone, anxious, angry and abandoned after her parent's divorce, aged 13. Her father moved far away and her mother had a breakdown and became angry and abusive. Due to the fear of not wanting to push her father any further away or aggravate her mother and face the repercussions. Nicola learnt to bury her anger, frustration and loneliness inside, causing her to carry this pain with her well into her twenties.

All she really wanted at the time was someone to talk to, someone who could help her through it and encourage her to focus on the future. But no one was there. Through reflection and coaching, Nicola became aware that the support she craved for, was also exactly what her mother needed during and after the divorce. Strategies to cope with the financial, logistical and emotional changes. Tips to deal with the stress, frustration, hurt and co-parenting challenges she was facing.

Having managed to have pulled herself out of the pit of depression, release the repressed anger, emotionally heal, design and create her dream life. Nicola decided she would help others do the same. It took Nicola a decade to heal and move on and her dream is to share the tools so her clients get results in months not years.

Nicola began supporting others in 2003 where she worked as a volunteer for four years with the Samaritans (a UK charity) where she listened to callers going through emotional distress and provided a safe place for them to share their feelings and thoughts.

Then in 2007, Nicola started her plan to work as a private coach, where she now supports individuals, couples and teenagers all across the globe via Skype or retreat packages in Dubai, to emotionally heal and make positive life changes.

Nicola studied Psychology, Sociology and Social Work and holds a Bsc (hons) in Sociology from the University of Bath. She is a UK certified grief and loss specialist with programs for adults to support themselves and their children through losses such as divorce.

Nicola is committed to getting transformational results for her clients and continues to learn and strengthen her practice. She is certified in many different disciplines (Coaching, NLP, Hypnotherapy, Myer Briggs, Time Line Therapy™, Relationship Coaching, Addiction Recovery, Cellular, DNA Healing, The Journey™, Family Therapy and Conflict Resolution.

Nicola draws on her experiences to offer encouragement, resilience skills and a unique perspective on how to turn marriage problems and divorce into an opportunity for growth and to jumpstart a new beginning.

BUSINESS: Pure Peace Coaching

WEBSITE: www.purepeacecoaching.com

EMAIL: nicola@purepeacecoaching.com

PHONE: +971 50 94 54 233

FACEBOOK: www.facebook.com/nicolabeerdxb/

TWITTER: www.twitter.com/nicolabeer1

INSTAGRAM: www.instagram.com/nicolabeer1/

YOUTUBE: www.youtube.com/channel/UCzEIXL16a4u_phWeKmrxJlQ

CHAPTER NINE

How to Work on Your Marriage When It No Longer Works

by Sara Freed

"The most powerful gift you can give your children is to invest your time and energy in relationship education." — Sara Freed

You're likely reading this chapter because you believe divorce has become an impending reality that you've thought long and hard about, but would like to know you've exhausted every potential remedy before making a final decision. Or, you're in—or plan to be in—a new relationship, and you don't want to repeat the same mistakes that led to the breakdown of your previous relationship. This chapter was written to help you repair wounds, heal, and forgive.

Sara Freed knows firsthand how difficult it can be when your "real" life doesn't turn out the way you thought it would—whether that means a divorce or a struggling marriage. Employing proven methods and techniques to help individuals and couples who are grappling with everything from the "should I get a divorce?" to "help me save my marriage", or starting anew if all efforts for salvaging their marriage fail, Sara approaches relationship coaching with compassion and sensitivity.

Sara draws on years of personal and professional experience to help you get the most from your relationship; how to survive conflict and thrive after facing adversity. Sara has gone through divorce and since remarried; drawing on her experiences, she has developed actionable strategies to manage conflict in a healthy way and build a solid foundation to enjoy a relationship filled with love, mutual respect, and happiness.

No doubt, not every relationship can be saved. If your spouse is incapable of compromise, unwilling to take any responsibility for their role in the breakdown of the relationship, is emotionally or physically abusive, you may not have the ability or desire to save your relationship. However, if you and your spouse are open and committed to making it work, or you want to acquire the skills to build a new relationship bound for success, you'll find Sara's insights invaluable.

In this chapter, Sara shares valuable tips and strategies including:

- How to identify the foundations of a healthy marriage
- How to appreciate and love one another
- How to recover, heal, and forgive
- How to manage conflict and protect your children
- How to find the right therapist or coach

Sara is based in Brooklyn, New York, where she is a Certified Divorce Coach (CDC). Sara also received clinical training at the Gottman Institute Clinical Training and with Michele Weiner-Davis's "Divorce Busting Intensive Workshop for Professionals".

Meet Sara

Jeremy Kossen: Sara, thank you for taking the time to share your insights. While most people reading this book may have already decided the points of contention in their marriage are irreconcilable, you offer a message of hope. You believe many marriages, where divorce seems inevitable, can not only be saved, but with the commitment and determination of both partners, wounds can be repaired and the marriage can thrive.

Can you share a little bit about what you do and the people you help?

Sara Freed: I'm a certified marriage coach. I educate people who are either at the pre-marital stage or a stage where they are experiencing considerable conflict. They may be considering divorce, but they have a desire to try to make their marriage work.

I help couples and individuals recognize what having a great and everlasting marriage entails. The methods I teach are simple, enabling anyone to learn and implement them.

You're clearly very passionate about what you do. Can you share with us what inspired you to go into this field of work?

I believe most marriages in crisis today can be saved from divorce, and I also believe the reason for the growing divorce rate is a lack of education as to what being married actually entails. If adults would invest the time and effort to acquire the knowledge of what makes for a good, happy, and everlasting marriage, the divorce rate would be significantly lower. As Michele Weiner-Davis terms it in Divorce Busting Methods, "Whoever said that marriage doesn't come with instructions?" Well, it does, and everyone can learn them. Learning it and practicing it will result in a harmonious marriage.

I'd like to share my insight based on my life experience. My first marriage of ten years, which resulted in three beautiful children, unfortunately, ended in divorce primarily due to the fact that my then husband strayed from our Orthodox Jewish religious path. We, as adults and parents, must strive to provide stability on all levels to our children, including religious values, regardless of which religion we're practicing. The parent deciding to change must respect that the children and the spouse can't be expected to change in accordance as well. Had I had the relationship insight and education I have today, I could have lovingly encouraged him to reconsider and thus avoided so much anguish and pain to all involved, specifically the children. And I strongly believe my marriage could have been saved.

I like what you said: it doesn't matter what faith or background you come from.

Exactly. It does not matter which religion you're practicing. It is universal.

Build (or Rebuild) a Happy, Healthy Marriage

Can you describe the foundation of a healthy marriage?

A healthy marriage foundation boils down to some basic principles. I will enumerate about ten that are crucial. I'll go into detail on the first two, and then briefly identify the remaining eight.

One- You need to know each other.

Be tuned in—knowledge is power. We need to invest the time frequently enough to be curious and ask each other things with regards to our likes, dislikes, hobbies, sensitivities, history, thoughts, wishes, et cetera. This enables spouses to know how to support the good things—the dreams within one another—and how to avoid hurting each other by knowing each other's sensitivities and history. Another benefit of knowing each other is it helps to keep the connection alive, allowing us to have things to talk about aside from the day-to-day goings-on.

Some people ask, "How do we do this?" And there are many ways. Luckily many thought leaders in couples counseling developed games for helping couples come up with the right questions to ask and helping them dig deep into each other's history. I have a link on my website in the store section (www.sarafreed.com/the-marriage-store) to the Gottman's Couples Retreat Game, which includes the Love Maps and Open Ended Questions card decks. Both are great tools for getting to know your partner on deeper and more meaningful levels, or you can come up with your own questions.

Two- Share "appreciations" and "admirations."

Express what you're grateful for. Don't allow your ego to get in the way. We are often too proud to let our partner be aware and know how much better off we are because of him or her. That's a shame. Everyone has a need to feel valued. Your partner needs to feel their good efforts and positive actions toward you and the family are recognized and meaningful. The founders of Imago Couples Therapy conclude that the lack thereof can make the difference between couples staying together versus ultimately drifting apart. Expressing appreciations and admirations are that powerful.

> *"Everyone has a need to feel valued. Your partner needs to feel their good efforts and positive actions toward you and the family are recognized and meaningful."*

An additional benefit of sharing your appreciations and admirations is that it will encourage your spouse to do more of what you admire and what you need, so that's a gain for you right there. Plus, it helps to keep you in a positive perspective versus being negative all the time about the relationship. We need to be consciously positive in order to be happy.

The other eight are:

- Character refinement
- Caring behaviors
- Consistent connection
- Managing marital conflicts,
- Helping each other's life dreams come true
- Developing and maintaining shared meanings
- Building trust
- Maintaining a strong commitment

Those are great! Some seem obvious, but I can see how it's easy to forget them or become complacent. Now that you've identified the elements and foundation of a strong marriage, can you share how a couple that has gone through (or is going through) considerable strife or conflict rebuild?

Some important components are:

Commit.

Commit to doing the work by learning and then practicing the newly learned methods.

Seal your exits.

By "seal your exits", I mean, don't discuss your issues with others. We tend to speak to our friends, our family, our neighbors, everybody, and anybody, but generally, they can't really help you—they are considered exits. Keep the discussion of your relationship within your relationship or with a professional. Another example of an exit is secluding oneself or busying yourself, thus avoiding your spouse. You need to spend time together and actively work on positive habits to bring about change because what you're really trying to do is connect.

Perseverance.

> *"It took time to develop the bad habits and poor behaviors. And it will take time to replace them with the new and better ways. It gets easier as it becomes habitual, but it does take time."*

It took time to develop the bad habits and poor behaviors. And it will take time to replace them with the new and better ways. It gets easier as it becomes habitual, but it does take time. You should expect some relapse as you move forward, but keep going in spite of the slip backs; through perseverance, you will ultimately win each other back and enjoy a satisfying, everlasting marriage.

Forgiveness.

Many people ask,

"Can I ever forgive?"

"Will he or she ever forgive?"

It will happen. It will take time. But, rest assured, you will get there. Be patient.

Recovery, Healing, and Forgiveness

Time heals, of course, but is there anything we can do to speed up the healing process? Forgiveness can be hard. Beyond allowing time to heal, how can we forgive our partner when they've done something that seems unforgivable?

How do we forgive? The first thing is to gain an understanding as to the underlying cause of why something happened. When we listen to what actually brought about a certain behavior, we gain a new perspective and thus, can more readily forgive as a result of a newfound understanding.

For example, consider an affair situation. Normally, I tell couples that, although there is no excuse for it, I do find more often than not that the affair developed out of a lingering and deep dissatisfaction with an unmet need from the spouse. If we're dissatisfied in a marriage, the spouse must not be fulfilling certain needs for the other one. When I say forgiveness takes time, that's because it takes time to unearth the "why." I'll go back to the idea that knowledge is power—knowing the reasons and taking responsibility for our own contribution in allowing for the rift to happen is a step forward toward forgiveness and healing.

Can you clarify what you mean when you say, "the spouse must not be fulfilling certain needs for the other one?"

Clearly, it's not the responsibility of one spouse if the other decides to cheat because we each are responsible for our own behavior, but we all contribute to strife. Everyone has a part in the problems at hand, as much as we don't want to take a look at ourselves. One of the things I do in coaching couples is explore each partner's individual contribution to the problem at hand. It's usually a huge eye opener for the client. When the client realizes and admits that perhaps "Yes, my spouse has strayed, but I was busying myself with everything and anything else other than giving my spouse the attention he/she needed and frequently asked for. I really didn't take it seriously." That's what I mean by the contribution. Not that you are to blame, but there might be something you've done to contribute to the problem. Figuring that out allows one to work on fixing the cause going forward. Thus, forgiveness comes forth when you realize that no one is 100% to blame. That's why it takes time.

That makes sense. We don't get anywhere if we just play the blame game. Sara, in the work you do with couples, what sort of process do you follow?

Normally, when one of the spouses contacts me, I have an initial consultation just to discover if we're a fit. When I meet with a client at the onset, I help them achieve clarity as to the current state of their marriage. I aim to discover their contribution to the problems with their spouse from their perspective and any external factors that may be affecting the situation. I accomplish this through specific coaching tools I learned from training with the CDC Divorce Coaching based in Florida.

When the client is seriously considering divorce and they're seeing divorce as the only option, another thing I do is walk down both paths with them. We walk down the path of saving the marriage, see what that would look like, and we analyze all the different aspects in detail. Then we walk down the path of what divorce would look like, and analyze all the different aspects they need to take into consideration. I utilize powerful questioning techniques that are very thought provoking, which helps broaden the client's perspective. My clients always discover new possibilities they hadn't even thought about before. When we continue working together, let's say to save the marriage, I utilize different couple's therapy modalities, like the Gottman modality. I also often use Imago and a lot of Michele Weiner's "Divorce Busting Methods".

Having shared your beliefs and how you do what you're doing, can you share how you bring your vision to life?

I see clients individually or as a couple. By doing one-on-one marriage coaching, I'm able to salvage many marriages. My clients learn about me via word of mouth, through social media, et cetera. The other thing I do, which I love, is pre-marital coaching, because, again, I strongly believe the reason so many marriages fail is because of the lack of education as to what a good marriage entails. Pre-marital coaching is about getting the couples to recognize and know what makes for good marriages and gain a real understanding of how to utilize those tools and methods. I also conduct marriage workshops as a certified trainer in the Gottman's "The Seven Principles for Making Marriage Work". And I do workshops for couples who are in the divorce process to help them develop co-parenting skills to use during and after the divorce; the skills they gain help them shelter their children from any unnecessary pain or exposure to conflicts.

Sara, what would you say are some of the greatest misconceptions parents should be aware of about the potential impact divorce can have on their children?

I love this question because it speaks very closely to my heart—given what I realized was happening with my own children during my divorce. There's this common saying that children are resilient, and I think that's a major misconception people have. Put simply, resilience means having the capacity to recover quickly. When we think about it, are the children indeed recovering quickly? Their home is undone. They have to begin shifting between two different homes and sometimes even more if they're being shifted among grandparents' homes. And so many other changes that are happening in their life. I believe it's an insult to children to say they're resilient. I think the more accurate thing to say is that they are conforming to the new realities, but they don't necessarily fully recover from the undoing of their home.

Another misconception is the fact that parents think they will know when something is off or wrong with their child and that they'll be able to be supportive of their child throughout the entire process. In truth, the children have witnessed their parents' inability to handle their own emotions. The child can lose trust in the parent being the one to turn to so that often becomes another problem.

Then, there is the common thought of, "My children will be no worse off than everybody else who is not impacted by divorce." I believe strongly that that is not true. The children have experienced the trauma—divorce is a trauma—and of course, trauma has an effect. Therefore, your child will carry a burden that their peers from non-divorced homes do not carry.

You've made some great points especially on the point of resiliency. We know many of the issues people have in their relationships later in life can be traced back to childhood trauma, and I think that's an important point to consider. If a couple is still in the divorce consideration phase, but they are open and willing to try to save the marriage, what strategies can they use?

There are so many strategies one can implement to preserve the marriage, but I think first and foremost, go out and learn the tools of how to actually manage conflict in a non-destructive manner. That's number one, high on the list.

> *"First and foremost, go out and learn the tools of how to actually manage conflict in a non-destructive manner."*

Another good strategy is to create "we" time. This is critical. Couples need to set aside time for themselves together. I believe a couple needs to spend at least twenty to thirty minutes a day together just sharing what the day was like. This is also very valuable for children. It's healthy for children to see that their parents value their own unit. That means within the family unit, it's very healthy for children to see parents having their own "we" time.

In a previous conversation we had, you stressed that it is important for couples to address unresolved trauma or unresolved pain. Can you expound on this?

This is a big one. Very often, even if we take the time to educate ourselves on what makes for a good marriage, we get stuck. What I found when working with couples—and we learn about this a lot in the different marriage modalities—is the reason we often get stuck is because there's some pain or hurt that must be resolved.

To illustrate, let's say we eat a new food and we don't take well to it. Now we have an upset stomach and the food does not metabolize correctly. Similarly, you can't implement and practice the new tools if there's something wrong; there's something bothering you that is still undigested and needs to be dealt with.

One of the interventions I do with couples is called the "Aftermath of the Fight". It's a Gottman intervention. This intervention allows for couples to revisit a painful episode by talking about it from a third person point of view, like a reporter, and taking turns doing so. The benefit is that both really get to hear what the situation looked and felt like to the other partner and healing comes about as a result of that new perspective.

When we talk about "baggage" in a relationship, which can be unresolved pain and trauma, is this really just an excuse for not dealing with things?

Unresolved pain and trauma can be unrelated to the current relationship, but it often resurfaces when your spouse behaves in a certain manner; it reminds you of a previous trauma. The Imago modality talks a lot about the 90-10 Principle. Ninety percent of why your spouse is upset about certain things you're doing or not doing is because of some childhood hurt those actions bring to the surface, and 10% actually has to do with the spouse.

Dialogues are important, whether you're utilizing the Gottman "Aftermath of the Fight" or "Dreams Within" intervention or utilizing an Imago Dialogue intervention. Those dialogue tools are a healthy way to bring up why a person is bothered by something or a way to discover what the trauma actually is. Very often, the person will cry and dig deep and realize their pain has something to do with their childhood or with a previous relationship. Just the fact that one is aware that it has nothing to do with them, that the spouse's behavior has a connection to some earlier experiences, and thus sensitivities have developed, already appeases a lot of the strife and is healing to both the spouse that's hurting and the spouse that's finding out where that hurt is really coming from.

Ninety percent comes from previous traumas? That's a shocking number, but it makes a lot of sense.

Yes. The Imago Dialogue, developed by Dr. Harville Hendrix and Dr. Helen LaKelly Hunt was formulated through extensive study of psychological theories and clinical work with couples. It shows, that most conflicts that have a painful charge are only 10% about the present situation while 90% is related to some past wound which is causing pain in the present.

> *"Most conflicts that have a painful charge are only 10% about the present situation while 90% is related to some past wound which is causing pain in the present."*

It often seems if a couple does end up getting divorced, that a lot of transference can emerge and the other parent can become a target to channel all that hurt, anguish, and anger from their unresolved trauma.

If they trace it back, the transference probably has something to do with a childhood pain. They may trace it to a previous relationship, but if they take the time to trace it fully, they may realize, they went wrong in the previous relationship because of traumas and childhood wounds they didn't deal with or face.

> *"We need to realize how much our childhood really impacts the rest of our lives... "*

We need to realize how much our childhood really impacts the rest of our lives and why we should be very keen on maintaining a healthy marriage and home environment for our children—or, in the case of a divorce, a healthy and civil co-parenting relationship.

I couldn't agree more, and too often we forget this.

Managing Conflict and Protecting Our Children

Now, when it comes to relationships, we know we will encounter conflict, but it's how we deal with or manage conflict. What suggestions do you have on how parents can insulate their children from this inevitable conflict and provide healthy modeling?

I love this question. First, I must say the part of the question I love is the fact that you mentioned "inevitable conflict". Conflict indeed is inevitable, but combat is a choice and that's not a choice one should ever take.

Create boundaries. Some examples of boundaries are as follows:

- Don't argue in front of your children. If you and your spouse are experiencing conflict, go into an office or go into your room.

- Eliminate threats like, "I'm leaving the relationship".

- Don't yell, as this is a form of violence.

- Don't name-call.

- Don't raise other issues—stick to the issue on hand.

- Dialogue, don't monologue. This is really important; make sure you are actually having a dialogue, not a monologue. This entails both partners taking turns to talk and LISTENING to the other as they work toward a resolution.

- And, finally, recognize you don't have to react to your spouse even if he or she is not behaving properly.

Let's say you are attending a couple of marriage coaching sessions. Then one day your husband comes home and yells at you for not preparing dinner on time, and you get so upset you start yelling back at him. You have a choice to react or not. Never, ever react just because your spouse is behaving in a wrong manner, especially when your children are around.

I have my clients imagine an invisible space between their partner's action and their reaction. That space is called choice. You have a choice of how you will react. Even if your spouse is going off on you and screaming and yelling, just take a deep breath and don't get sucked into a fight and argument, especially if you are in front of the children. The greatest gift we can give our children is modeling to them what a healthy, loving, and caring relationship looks like. If we do so, then our children will know how to behave in their marriage. For this alone, it's worth our restraint to be proper role models as marriage partners.

These are all great points you make. And I especially like how you distinguish "conflict" versus "combat". Conflict is inevitable, but combat is a choice, and it's a choice we should never make. There are other healthier ways to manage and deal with the conflict at hand.

That's exactly right.

As parents, what are some things we can learn from our children?

There's a lot we can learn from children. You know the saying "from the mouth of babes"? Children are very blunt. They're not busy with their egos, and we can see that when we observe kindergarten children. Anybody teaching kindergarten children or watching children play with their playmates at the age of two, three, et cetera, will see that when a child wants to be someone's friend, they'll just go over and say, "Can you please be my friend?" As adults, we're shy. We're busy with the ego. We wouldn't do that. We tend to not ask for what we want simply by just stating it. I'll give you an example. I'll give you an example from something that happened with my own 2-1/2-year-old grandchild.

I was walking my daughter to the door after a brief visit to my house. My grandchild was in the carriage. As I walked her through the door, I gave her a kiss and I said, "Goodbye. Have a great day." My cute little grandson piped up and said, "Me, too, grandma. Me, too, grandma," and he gestured to his cheek and he said, "Kiss, kiss!" He wanted a kiss, too. Of course, I smothered him with kisses. As I walked away, I said to myself, "Wow, look at that. He really embodied what I teach couples," and that is; say what you mean, mean what you say, and don't say it in a mean way. Just simply state your need. Like he said, "Grandma, I'd like to have a kiss," and he got that. Instead of stating in a negative matter what we're not getting—for example, "You never help me with the dishes"—simply say, "I would love for you to help me with the dishes." Doing things in this manner will actually help couples get what they want from one another.

That's great advice, Sara. I don't know why we forget that from when we're kids. So often we don't say what we mean or, even worse, we don't communicate anything at all. We withdraw or suppress a problem. Then it gets bottled up, and we never deal with the issue. Or worse, it erupts out of nowhere like a volcano.

Right, either we don't express it or what happens most often is we express a need in a negative manner: "I'm so upset you don't take out the garbage. I've reminded you ten times," or "I'm really upset you're late again," instead of saying, "Honey, it would mean so much for me if you came home on time. If you can't, please call me next time just to let me know." Just simply state what you need.

Finding the Right Therapist

I think who we choose as a therapist or coach is so important. Sara, could you provide a few tips on how to find the right professional?

This is a great question. When couples come to me, I find they've been to so many therapists prior to seeing me. I'm usually the last stop, so I began digging to find out why, and I think often couples don't know what to look for in a therapist or how to find someone who truly shares their values.

The most important advice I can give to readers is to make sure the therapist or coach you see is somebody who's trained in marriage counseling modalities. It doesn't matter whether you're seeing a therapist or a coach, they must be trained in couple's counseling modalities. It doesn't matter if the therapist or coach has some letters after their name; that doesn't mean much. The MSW, the CSW, Ph.D., et cetera, they don't matter if they were not trained in specific marriage modalities. Some of the best modalities are Imago and Gottman. And Michele Weiner-Davis, for example, is internationally acclaimed and the director of the Divorce Busting Center in Colorado. She promotes powerful divorce busting methods, which I am trained in.

The other thing I suggest is to see a marriage professional who takes a holistic approach and is family oriented—one who doesn't view you as an individual, but sees you as part of a whole. Meaning, you are part of your spouse and your children, and they take all these different people into consideration when working with you.

Very often, one person comes to me and the spouse is not yet ready to see me. I keep in mind that there are other people in the picture. If there are children involved, I keep the children in mind. I continue doing my work using that holistic approach, and that's something clients should find out about from the respective coach or therapist they'll be working with.

I'm very keen on sharing insight about the fact that, very often, therapists or coaches will encourage one of the spouses to see another therapist for their individual work. I find this can be very detrimental because that individual therapist might have an entirely different method or derail the spouse from the marriage work they're doing in the couple's therapy.

There are exceptions to the rule, one would be addictions. Addiction is a very specific modality, so if one of the spouses might need to see an addiction therapist, whether it's sex addiction, gambling addiction, or any other addiction, I believe that that will not derail the spouse, because it's a very specific therapy and can be a good enhancement to the couple's work they're doing.

Let's say you have a dynamic in the relationship and you're dealing with a marriage coach that you share, but there are certain things that

perhaps the husband or the wife want to talk to somebody else to get things off their chest. Do you suggest support groups or are there other things you recommend in that situation?

I would still recommend they use the same counselor or coach for their individual work and relationship work. For example, sometimes I see both the husband and wife individually outside of our couples' work, because I think the marriage counselor or coach working with the couple has the best—and the most—insight into what the individual work might be and how they can best help that person individually in a way which will enhance the person, the couple, and the marriage. I strongly believe that very often one or both partners need to have some individual work done, but it's better done with that same marriage counselor or coach. I think that keeps it within the realm of the work being done as a couple and not being diverted or misled by other advice. However, there are times when we need to refer the client to a specialist, depending on what the issue is.

I think a lot of people don't really realize there are coaches and therapists who are open to doing both couples and individual sessions. I think you bring up some very valid points, particularly that it may not be beneficial to the relationship if each partner is seeing a different professional. They risk receiving conflicting messages being brought into their relationship that could potentially create more conflict rather than helping move towards resolving or managing that conflict.

Correct, you know the popular saying, "Too many cooks spoil the broth," and boy, I've seen that happen. That's why I'm very keen on making sure we keep it as tight as we can in terms of how many therapists my clients see.

Sara helps couples build great marriages defined by mutual satisfaction, respect, and love, and to enjoy healthy and happy family lives. She offers a free initial 30-minute consultation. To learn more and download her free report, "5 Secrets to Bring Peace and Happiness to Your Marriage", visit Sara's website, www.SaraFreed.com.

ABOUT SARA FREED

Based in Brooklyn, New York, Sara Freed is a relationship and divorce coach who works with individuals, couples, and families who are struggling with marital and relationship issues. Sara knows firsthand how difficult it can be when your "real" life doesn't turn out the way you thought it would – whether that means a divorce or a struggling marriage. Sara has learned proven methods and techniques to help individuals who are grappling with every stage—from the "should I?" to "help me save my marriage" or starting anew if all efforts for salvaging a marriage fail.

Sara was inspired to do the work she does based on her own life's experiences. Her first marriage resulted in three beautiful children – but ended after ten years. During her ten years as a single parent, she struggled with lingering divorce issues, single and co-parenting, community expectations and life obligations. Despite her divorce, she has been blessed to see her children grow into fine adults.

With her "now" wonderful husband, Sara was determined not just to stay married, but to stay happily married. As a result, she has dedicated herself to learn all she can about what makes marriages great and how one can indeed attain and sustain that. She furthered her research and passion by obtaining certifications from thought leaders in marriage/couples counseling and divorce coaching and implementing tried and true techniques in her practice along with the school of hard knocks – lessons learned from her own journey.

In coaching couples and divorcees, Sara has found her true calling. She is passionate about helping others by sharing what she's learned through her life experience and relationship education. Add in her persistent optimism and "get it done" attitude, and you have a person who is uniquely qualified to guide you through your marriage problems or divorce.

Sara is a Certified Divorce Coach (CDC) who has also trained at the Gottman Institute Clinical Training and with Michele Weiner-Davis's "Divorce Busting Intensive Workshop for Professionals"

BUSINESS: Sara Freed

WEBSITE: www.sarafreed.com

EMAIL: sara@sarafreed.com

PHONE: 917-355-8630

LOCATION: Brooklyn, NY

FACEBOOK: www.facebook.com/sarafreedcoaching/

TWITTER: www.twitter.com/jfamilycoach

LINKEDIN: www.linkedin.com/in/sarafreed

INSTAGRAM: www.instagram.com/sarafreedcoach/

PINTEREST: www.pinterest.com/sara_freed/

CHAPTER TEN

Guilt-Free Parenting in Divorce
by Cherie D. Morris

"It's not the mistakes we make with our children that determines how they remember us, but how we repair those mistakes that matters to them."

— *Cherie Morris*

After her long-term marriage ended in divorce, Cherie—a mother of four—became inspired to explore how to help other parents going through what is too often a chaotic and stressful life transition, create an experience that is fairer, cooperative and serves the best interests of the children and adults. Cherie's life experiences—personal, professional and academic—inspired her to employ rational thinking accompanied by an ability to empathize and compromise in order to achieve successful results.

In addition to being a Certified Divorce Coach (CDC), Cherie Morris is a lawyer, certified yoga teacher, mother, and writer. Cherie's legal training enables her to take a logical and reasoned approach to issues. She began exploring alternate dispute resolution and transformative mediation in order to understand how to change the nature of conflict and improve dynamics when conflict occurs, when a solely rational approach may not succeed.

Recognizing that a divorce agreement is an important contract that requires each party to consider the long-term consequences of taking specific actions now, Cherie believes it is vitally important to not only understand and analyze each decision in divorce carefully, and rationally, but with a strong consideration for who you want to be in line with your values. It is also important to contemplate the relationship that will continue with a former spouse well into the future, especially when there are minor children involved.

Re-partnered, Cherie is a proud mother and part of a domestic partnership with a wonderful man. They live in Washington D.C. with their blended family that now includes five children, two of whom are in college.

Meet Cherie

Jeremy: Cherie, recently you launched a new project, Dear Divorce Coach. What is the goal of Dear Divorce Coach and how can it help people going through a divorce?

Cherie: Dear Divorce Coach is a collaboration with my business partner Vicki Vollweiler. We created the website to be a place where you can go to find much of the information you need to navigate the often confusing, chaotic world of separation and divorce.

On our website—www.DearDivorceCoach.com—we feature advice on how to get legal help, manage your financial matters, navigate the emotional issues in divorce, parenting and how to get support for it, and a lot more. We feature a divorce advice column too. If people have questions about separation, divorce, post-divorce complications, parenting—almost anything related to the world of divorce—they can ask a coach and we will answer any questions you may have. We really like for people to ask questions because divorce can be a confusing and overwhelming process and sometimes it's hard to find the answers you're looking for when you need them. We wanted to make Dear Divorce Coach a real access point for people by making it easy to navigate and offering resources. Often, we are available when others are not.

How did you get started and what inspired you to become a divorce coach?

I am educated as a lawyer and I practiced law for a long time. After I experienced my own divorce, with four children, I realized there really were no go-to resources in divorce. Certainly you can find a lawyer—and I have access to good lawyers and to good professionals in the field—but there is more than just the legal part of the divorce. You find that you rely on a relatively small network of people to mostly tell you what to do. That is not a great approach to a significant life event. It is important to calm the chaos and overwhelm so that the individual can decide how to proceed. They and their children are the ones to live with the consequences of divorce for a very long time. It should not be about someone else's value judgments imposed upon them.

After my own experience, I wanted to help people find a way through their divorce that I really wasn't able to when I experienced it. I decided to put my legal hat on, my rational mode, combine it with my experience teaching yoga and my writing experience into one field. I saw divorce coaching as a real fit and proceeded to get the certification for it.

It's interesting you mention yoga—divorce can be one of the most stressful and traumatic events in a person's life and I can imagine that incorporating yoga would be very therapeutic. How do you incorporate yoga into Dear Divorce Coach?

We produce an ongoing series of yoga videos that are available on our website such as "Managing Stress in Separation and Divorce" and "Yoga for Stress Relief in Divorce." We created the videos to help people relax, sit quietly, do breathing exercises and meditate. While there is no series of postures that cure all the ills of divorce, yoga can certainly provide all of us with a respite from the worries and concerns we have when going through a divorce. It also gives us tools to access when we are experiencing the most stressful parts of it.

Managing Anxiety and Overwhelm

What kind of outcomes do you seek to help your clients achieve through your work with them, both short-term and long-term?

In the short term, we seek to help people lower the threshold of anxiety, of chaos, and the idea that this is unmanageable. The way my partner Vicki and I do that is to provide information and resources in an organized, easily digestible fashion. If you throw too much material or too many resources at people all at once, it can be as useless as giving them nothing at all. We present the information in a way that makes sense for their particular situation. We tailor our coaching to their specific needs.

Through our individual and online coaching programs, we provide a path for people to follow. We say to them, "Start at A and you will end up at Z. It may not feel like you will, but we can help you get there through coaching. We can help you put all those pieces together in a logical way." We help them create their vision. And, we provide the path so that they have a framework to get there.

> *"In the heat of divorce, parents can easily confuse what they think they want with what will ultimately be best for their children and themselves."*

As coaches, we act as objective thinking partners and help people stay accountable to their values so they can achieve their goals. People need gentle reminders such as, "Are you considering your own needs now? Are you thinking about the continuing relationship you need with your soon-to-be ex? Are you sincerely thinking about putting your kids first?" In the heat of divorce, parents can easily confuse what they think they want with what will ultimately be best for their children and themselves. I believe for all of us, a key long-term goal is that we have what we need in our relationships moving forward and we have the kind of relationships we desire. When you have children, this is even more important, because the reality is, you will have a lifelong relationship with your ex.

I agree. It's so important we remember that through our children, we're connected to our ex for life. Irrespective of the divorce, there will always be a relationship that exists.

When you begin the negotiations that are inevitable as part of the divorce, it's easy to lose sight of that. But, if you focus on long term goals and follow a framework, you can maintain that larger worldview. If we can help people do that, then I think we've succeeded as divorce coaches. That's what Vicki and I try to do through Dear Divorce Coach.

Aligning Values and Goals with Our Behavior

Can you share an example of a client you've worked with how you helped them?

We've seen many clients with a variety of different issues, but one client I'll focus on is a woman I'll call, Mindy. When Mindy came to us, she felt an extreme amount of guilt at the prospect of getting a divorce. She was concerned that as her children grew up after the divorce, she would not be able to provide the home she felt they deserved. Or, they would be perceived negatively as being from a divorced family which would severely and negatively impact their lives. And finally, she worried she would deprive her kids materially, as she wouldn't be able to provide them with all the things they needed. Because she was obviously in a state of worry, the first thing we did with Mindy was to discuss her goals for the future. We asked her what it was she really wanted at the end of the day and at the end of her divorce, which was going to happen whether she wanted it or not.

As we helped her clarify her values, what we discovered— and again, these are her values, not ours—is that what she really wanted was to make sure she had time with her kids and they understood she had a very good work ethic, that she could provide for them in the way she intended to, and that they could grow up knowing they had a role model in their mother. Of course, this all points to the fact that what was scariest to Mindy was the unknown. She thought it was all very overwhelming and unknowable. What Vicki and I did was help her see that you can make a plan for the future. It may not go exactly as you intend, but if you start on the front end by determining who you are and want to be, then you can follow that framework for every decision you have to make.

"With a plan in place, Mindy was able to calm her nerves, as well as quiet the guilt she had been experiencing as a Mom in a failing marriage."

With a plan in place, Mindy was able to calm her nerves, as well as quiet the guilt she had been experiencing as a Mom in a failing marriage. She remembered, once she calmed the overwhelm, that she is a good parent. She was able to provide for her children, and learned that it wasn't really the material stuff they wanted or needed, but time with their mom. Mindy developed a mindset to proceed with a separation that she did not initially want. In the end she found a way to serve her best interests, the children's best interests, and even some of her soon-to-be ex's.

I imagine Mindy's situation is quite common, and I know that many parents deal with feelings of guilt. How do you help parents overcome feelings of guilt?

There are a couple of things that can be done, Jeremy. For one, feelings are not actions. It's certainly okay to have lots of feelings—we all do. We have lots of feelings every day. But, just because you have a feeling, doesn't mean you have to act upon it.

One strategy Vicki and I coach clients to use is to pay attention to their feelings. Acknowledging the feeling first is important. They can then focus on becoming the person they want to be. We refer clients to mental health professionals as necessary, of course. However, much of what occurs in divorce can lead to feelings which are situational and coaching can and does help.

We use values exercises to help clients understand what it is they want for themselves and for their children. These techniques help alleviate what some call the guilt of divorce. Once clients see and are able to clarify what they want going forward in their lives, they're able to set the guilt aside.

One of our tips to people includes that old adage: "Take things one day at a time." We help them find a framework for the long run. Then they are able to live each day, to take each day and each situation, and place it in line with the value systems they consciously created in their work with us. That way, they can feel confident, instead of afraid, each and every day.

We know men and women—fathers and mothers— process emotions differently, and since you work with both, can you share an example of a father you've worked with who encountered a similar situation—or a situation in which the father may have needed a bit of encouragement to help him stay focused on what was most important for his children and their relationship?

Vicki and I believe our practice and what we do at Dear Divorce Coach is as much about supporting men, as it is about supporting women However, we sometimes find men are more reluctant to seek the help they may need. They tend to be less friendly to the idea of joining community groups. For whatever reason, they're still not often socialized to do it.

When men in need of support reach out to us, we very much want to support him. Recently, Vicki and I had a client that we'll call Henry. He was a successful middle-aged professional who was surprised and terrified when his wife asked for a divorce. He tried to reconcile with her, but that didn't work.

After his reconciliation efforts were unsuccessful, Henry decided that his wife—his soon-to-be ex—was an enemy. This became his framework and how he understood the world. He had been successful in business; he had many friends and enemies. These factors helped shape his worldview, so when his wife decided to leave him, he viewed this as a betrayal, and that she was now his enemy. He was forgetting one thing, though—he would still need to co-parent with her. At first, Henry allowed the focus of the divorce to consume and dominate him, and initially he did not recognize he and his ex-spouse needed to still work together for the benefit of the kids. When he first came to see us, he couldn't understand how to shift this mindset. He saw himself as a victim. He originally came to us because he couldn't get a negotiation with her that he wanted and this frustrated him. At his wits end about what to do, he came across an article on divorce coaching and finally decided to reach out.

When Henry called us, we asked him to do an exercise around who he wanted to be to see if the actions he was taking with his soon-to-be ex, and on behalf of his children, were in line with his own values. Although he didn't really want to admit it at first, Henry had created a whole mindset around the way he was behaving. Through coaching, he came to understand that all the animosity he had for his ex, all the hurt, was about his own emotional devastation. He needed some professional therapy to help with what may have caused him to behave in this manner and to address the anxiety and depression that had been prevalent in the marriage too. However, it was Coaching that helped him see he could break out of his single-minded victim status and behave differently in order to successfully achieve a positive outcome with his soon-to-be ex and his children.

> *"Through coaching, he came to understand that all the animosity he had for his ex, all the hurt, was about his own emotional devastation."*

We helped Henry understand that the way he was behaving was not truly in line with how he wanted to behave as a father. He felt terribly guilty that he had failed his kids. His own parents were divorced and he was afraid there was no other path but to be an enemy to his ex. He didn't know what else to do. After he came to understand that he wanted to behave differently, this helped him shift his mindset and move forward. We helped him elicit positive behavioral changes by asking him how he thought he could best approach the issue of getting what he most wanted—more time with the kids. He recognized that he had an opportunity to make an offer to his soon-to-be ex— to give her what she wanted with the kids—by simply focusing on what was in the kids' best interest.

Henry started to recognize that even the way he transitioned the kids between homes might not serve their best interest. The kids had some reservations about being picked up by one parent at the other parent's home, so he started to change that. As he did, he saw that his soon-to-be ex-spouse was more receptive to the things he asked for and the things he wanted for his children too.

A key lesson we can draw from Henry's situation is that mindset can keep parents from achieving their goals, particularly their parenting goals. We see this with a lot of people, not just men. When we help them shift that focus—either through value exercises or work around goals—they can change their behaviors to align with values. They can move away from all the shame and guilt they may have felt in the divorce, especially if they're also getting some sort of therapeutic support if required. During a divorce, this kind of coaching can make a significant difference, because it goes beyond whatever therapeutic issues may exist, and helps free people to behave differently and prioritize their kids.

That's a great example, Cherie, and it really underscores how helpful divorce coaching can be by enabling us to the develop self-awareness required to align our values and goals with our behaviors and what's best for our children.

From your experience, what would you say are some of the most important things for parents to consider through the divorce process?

When you're raising a child, there are numerous factors to consider, but you can boil it down to a couple of essentials. One is that kids are not really interested in what you can give them. They're interested in how you execute on what you do with them. Whether you have a lot of time in a day or a little bit of time, they want to feel that the time you spend with them is quality time, that you're really focusing on their interests and their needs. And frankly, parents want to do that. If you can begin to do that in a very conscious way with your kids and set aside that time for them, whether it's a few minutes or a few hours, then you are doing them a great service. What they want is time and attention from each parent. That allows them to understand that both parents love them and that they will have time from each parent, even if they live in two different households.

"Kids are not really interested in what you can give them. They're interested in how you execute on what you do with them."

Finding the Right Support Professionals

Many coaching and mediation professionals believe there is a lack of awareness in our society on how to best approach divorce, or what the best process is. Many people simply aren't aware there are far healthier alternatives to reflexively calling an attorney without even knowing what sort of philosophy that attorney embraces or whether they even have child-centric values. Most people don't realize that an attorney's role is to advance their client's position, irrespective of whether or not that position is best for their children.

Why does it seem so many people are unaware of their options and why do you feel it's important for parents to work with a professional, such as a coach like yourself, rather than just immediately going down that path of, "I'm going to hire the 'best' attorney I can afford"?

So many different professionals that do coaching or mediation find there are many options people don't consider, and it's often because they're overwhelmed or uninformed. Generally, our first step is to try to calm that feeling of overwhelm and help people recognize that you really do not want to set up an already adversarial dynamic in a more extreme fashion, especially when there are children who be impacted by your decisions. It's not that family law lawyers necessarily intend to promote conflict, but the nature of traditional litigation is that there is a perception that one person is right, and the other person is wrong. It's a win-lose dynamic.

If you consider alternatives to the adversarial nature of litigation, then you can work to serve the best interest of the adults and the children. For example, divorcing couples may hire a mediator or hire two separate mediators who can then work with each other. Or, they can hire a collaborative group where each lawyer works within their collaborative framework that includes parenting and financial professionals and therapeutic professionals too.

It's important to clear up a common misconception. Collaborative divorce is not without cost. People need to think about their individual situation and what will work for them. We work with clients to address those various scenarios. We ask them to interview various professionals and see what feels like a good fit for them emotionally and is within their financial means.

Sometimes you can find a family law lawyer who does everything they can to keep the divorce process as non- adversarial as possible. But, if that's the path you pick, you can't know what your soon-to-be ex will do and we advise that you be thoughtful throughout the process. We welcome clients to consider a less adversarial approach, and we are eager to advise them on the best way to proceed for themselves and their children.

Closing Thoughts

What tips or suggestions do you have for someone who is considering a therapist, attorney, or mediator?

Certainly you want to know about their credentials, and there are many places you can go to find credential information. Also, a great way to go about it is to get a referral from a professional or someone you know who has gone through a similar experience. The very best experiences I have had have been with clients who came to me through a referral. You may know someone who has had experience with a particular professional— it doesn't have to be your friend or family member. You can ask other professionals for referrals and what sort of experiences their clients have had. The best way to get a sense of the process with that professional is if other current or former clients are willing to speak to you on behalf of the practitioner. This is good practice whether you're talking about lawyers, parenting coordinators, financial professionals or therapists; it applies across the board.

In addition to Dear Divorce Coach, Cherie provides divorce and other life transition coaching to individuals and couples. Visit www. DearDivorceCoach.com to find a calendar of upcoming events and additional resources, including blogs, articles, videos, and an advice column. If you have questions about divorce, you can post your question anonymously through the Dear Divorce Coach homepage. You can email Cherie at coach@deardivorce.com or call her at (301)928-4695. Access Cherie's free guide on "How to Be the Best Parent You Can Be in Separation and Divorce" on Cherie's website.

ABOUT CHERIE D. MORRIS

In addition to being a Certified Divorce Coach (CDC), Cherie Morris is a lawyer, certified yoga teacher, mother, and writer. Cherie's legal training enables her to take an approach to issues that is logical and reasoned. She began exploring alternate dispute resolution and transformative mediation in order to understand how to change the nature of conflict and improve dynamics when conflict occurs, when a solely rational approach may not succeed.

Cherie had a long-term marriage, with children, which ended in divorce. This deepened her desire to explore how to make a very chaotic and stressful life transition a more organized, fair and cooperative one, when possible, in order to serve the best interests of children and adults. Cherie's life experiences – personal, professional and academic – inspired her to employ rational thinking accompanied by an ability to empathize and compromise in order to achieve successful results.

Recognizing that a divorce agreement is an important contract that requires each party to consider the long-term consequences of taking specific actions now, Cherie believes it is vitally important to not only understand and analyze each decision in divorce carefully, and rationally, but with a strong consideration for your best self and a relationship that may continue with a former spouse well into the future, especially when there are children involved.

Cherie has four children of her own, two of whom are in college, and is part of a blended family. She is delighted to include her partner's daughter and say they have a combined five. Life is always interesting and challenging.

In addition to her work with Dear Divorce Coach, Cherie is available for coaching sessions regarding divorce and other life transitions for individuals and couples too. She also has various DC-based support group opportunities available in conjunction with a licensed therapist.

Cherie graduated from Duke University and the University of Iowa College of Law. She worked as a lawyer from 1991 through 2003 and since that time has worn many hats: COO of a law firm, yoga teacher, and author.

BUSINESS: Dear Divorce Coach

WEBSITE: www.deardivorcecoach.com

WEBSITE: www.lifetransitionsmatter.com

EMAIL: cherie@deardivorcecoach.com

PHONE: 301.928.4695

LOCATION: Washington DC

FACEBOOK: www.facebook.com/DearDivorceCoach

TWITTER: www.twitter.com/DearDivorceTeam

LINKEDIN: www.linkedin.com/in/morrischerie

YOUTUBE: www.youtube.com/channel/UC_1-4c18vWODR8cvJ9B6Kxg

CHILDREN'S BILL OF RIGHTS: HOW WE WISH TO BE TREATED BY OUR PARENTS

(Source: Children's Rights Council)

"The Best Parent Is Both Parents"

We, the children of parents who have or about to end their relationship as we know it, deserve fair and just treatment by each of you. We ask you to consider us while we all go through the changes occurring within our family. To make it easy for you to think of us, we have agreed on some things that we think you should consider.

We are your children and we love each of you!

1. We need to be told that we are half of each of you and that you both love us, no matter what happens with your relationship.

2. We deserve to be treated as important people with our own ideas, feelings, wishes and not as property for one of you to "win".

3. We want to have our questions about our changing family answered respectfully, with age-appropriate answers that do not include you blaming or belittling each other.

4. We want to make our own judgments about each of our parents and to be allowed to love both of you without one degrading the other to us.

5. We want to learn from both of you about your religious ideas, hobbies, interests and experiences.

6. It hurts us to be asked or expected to take sides against one of you.

7. We never want to be made the method of our parents' communication by being asked to deliver messages back and forth.

8. We never want to be made a messenger by being told to carry notes, legal papers, money or anything else between you.

9. We want to never be asked to spy or to be interrogated about events in the other parent's home.

10. We want you to know that it hurts when you treat us like leverage in your fight.

Expression of Love

1. We want to enjoy continuing care and guidance from both of you; to be educated in mind, nourished in spirit and developed in body, in an environment of unconditional love.

2. We want to have a continuing relationship with both parents and be allowed to love both parents.

3. We want to be allowed to continue loving relationships with both grandparents and other extended family members and to be allowed to have them in our lives.

4. We want to be allowed to own and display pictures of both of our parents and family members.

Sense of Security

1. We deserve to have our parents work together toward our best interests at all times.

2. We need to have the sense of security that we get from loving homes and to be sheltered from harm.

3. We need to be able to spend quality time with each parent without the other interfering by making plans for us, offering us other things to do instead or threatening to punish us for what we did wrong by not allowing us to go with our other parent.

4. We deserve to live in an atmosphere where we won't be abused or neglected.

5. We are entitled to be happy children and not be involved in the conflict, problems and fighting of our parents.

6. We want to be allowed to have a place for our stuff when we're at each parent's home.

7. We need to have a daily and weekly routine that is predictable and that I can understand.

8. We wish that you would not burden us with adult duties and responsibilities. I cannot be expected to raise myself or my siblings. Though I may be able to help, I need you both to guide me.

9. We need to be able to communicate with the other parent and have private conversations without eavesdropping or recording or being told what to say or what not to say.

Freedom of Choice

1. We need to be told that our parents' divorce or separation is not our fault. We deserve to be comforted when we are scared of what's happening within our family.

2. We need to be allowed to live with each parent for extended periods of time, as situations will allow.

3. We must be allowed to choose to remain in sports, special classes or clubs that I like, without being made to feel guilty that my activities may conflict with your parenting time. If possible, join me in my activities.

Development of Self

1. We deserve to have parents who discuss my development and are interested in how I am progressing.

2. We must be allowed to discuss our feelings and emotions in appropriate ways with your understanding and love.

3. We need to have parents that listen to our problems and concerns, as well as our dreams and desires.

Time and Information

1. We need to be able to communicate with either parent as often as needed.

2. We need to enjoy appropriate Parenting Time access (visitation) with each parent that will serve our needs and preferences.

3. We need to know what is good about the other parent.

4. We need to have clear communications (even if only in writing) about medical treatments, psychological therapy, educational issues, accidents, illnesses and other important concerning us and our parents.

5. We need to have consistent and predictable boundaries in each parent's home especially if the rules in each house may significantly differ from the other.

6. We need to know in advance about decisions including living arrangements, transfer times and locations, holidays, summer schedules, and special circumstances.

7. We need to have educational, religious, athletic and other necessary persons informed about changes in family situation.

8. We need to have certain personal information about each parent kept private.

Last and foremost, we need each parent to be the adults in our new family structure and act accordingly.

Made in the USA
San Bernardino, CA
02 November 2017